Soldier Silhouet

Our Front

William L. Stidger

Alpha Editions

This edition published in 2023

ISBN : 9789357963480

Design and Setting By
Alpha Editions
www.alphaedis.com
Email - info@alphaedis.com

Contents

FOREWORD

Some human experiences that one has in France stand out like the silhouettes of mountain peaks against a crimson sunset. I have tried in this book to set down some of those experiences. I have had but one object in so doing, and that object has been to give the father and mother, the brother and sister, the wife and child and friend of the boys "Over There" an accurate heart-picture. I have not attempted the too great task of showing the soul of the soldier, although I have tried to picture him at some of his great moments when he forgets himself and rises to glorious heights, just as he might do at home if the opportunity called.

I have tried to show his experiences on the transports, when he lands in France, his welcome there, the reactions of the trench life; something of his self-sacrifice, his willingness to serve even unto the end; his courage, his sunshine. I have also given some other pictures of France that aim to show his heart-relations to his allies and to the folks at home.

If I have done this, sufficient shall be my reward.

I
SILHOUETTES OF SONG

The great transport was cutting its sturdy way through three dangers: the submarine zone, a terrific storm beating from the west against its prow, and a night as dark as Erebus because of the storm, with no lights showing.

I had the midnight-to-four-o'clock-in-the-morning "watch" and on this night I was on the "aft fire-control." Below me on the aft gun-deck, as the rain pounded, the wind howled, and the ship lurched to and fro, I could see the bulky forms of the boy gunners. There were two to each gun, two standing by, with telephone pieces to their ears, and six sleeping on the deck, ready for any emergency. The greatcoats made them look like gaunt men of the sea as they huddled against their guns, watching, waiting. I wondered what they could see in that impenetrable darkness, if a U-boat could even survive in that storm; but Uncle Sam never sleeps in these days, and this transport was especially worth watching, for it carried a precious cargo of wounded officers and men back to the homeland, west bound.

For an hour I had heard no sound from the boys on the gun-deck below me. When I was on watch in the daylight I knew them to be just a great crowd of fine, buoyant, happy American lads, full of pranks and play and laughter, but they were strangely silent to-night as the ship ploughed through the storm. The storm seemed to have made men of them. They were just boys, but American boys in these days become men overnight, and acquit themselves like men.

I watched their silent forms below me with a great feeling of wonderment and pride. The ship lurched as it swung in its zigzag course. Then suddenly I heard a sweet sound coming from one of the boys below me. I think that it was big, raw-boned "Montana" who started it. It was low at first and, with the storm and the vibrations of the ship, I could not catch the words. The music was strangely familiar to me. Then the boy on the port gun beside "Montana" took the old hymn up, and then the two reserve gunners who were standing by, and then the gunners on the starboard side, and I caught the old words of:

"Jesus, Saviour, pilot me
Over life's tempestuous sea;
    Unknown waves before me roll
    Hiding rock and treacherous shoal;
Chart and compass came from Thee;
Jesus, Saviour, pilot me."

Above the creaking and the vibrations of the great ship, above the beating of the storm, the gunners on the deck below, all unconsciously, in that storm-tossed night were singing the old hymn of their memories, and I think that I never heard that wonderful hymn when it sounded sweeter to me than it did then, as the second verse came sweetly from the lips and hearts of those gunners:

"As a mother stills her child
Thou canst hush the ocean wild;
Boistrous waves obey Thy will
When Thou sayst to them, 'Be still.'
Wondrous Sovereign of the sea,
Jesus, Saviour, pilot me."

We hear a good deal of how our boys sing "Hail! Hail! The Gang's All Here" and "Where Do We Go From Here, Boys?" as a ship is sinking. I know American soldiers pretty well. I do not know what they sang when the *Tuscania* went down, but I am glad to add my picture to the other and to say that I for one heard a crowd of American gunners singing "Jesus, Saviour, Pilot Me Over Life's Tempestuous Sea." The mothers and fathers of America must know that the average American boy will have the lighter songs at the end of his lips, but buried down deep in his heart there is a feeling of reverence for the old hymns, and whether he sings them aloud or not they are there singing in his heart; and sometimes, under circumstances such as I have described, he sings them aloud in the darkness and the storm.

If you do not believe this because you have been told so often by magazine correspondents, who see only the surface things, that all the boys sing is ragtime, let Bishop McConnell, of the Methodist Episcopal Church, tell you of that Sunday evening when, at the invitation of General Byng, he addressed, under the auspices of the Y. M. C. A., a great regiment of the Scottish Guards. That night, in a shell-destroyed stone theatre, he spoke to them on "How Men Die." In a week from that night more than two-thirds of them had been killed. When Bishop McConnell asked them what they would like to sing, this great crowd of sturdy, bare-kneed soldiers of democracy, who had borne the brunt of battle for three years, asked for "O God, Our Help in Ages Past."

Yes, I know that the boys sing the rag-time, but this must not be the only side of the picture. They sing the old hymns, too, and memories of nights "down the line," when I have heard them in small groups and in great crowds singing the old, old hymns of the church, have burned their silhouettes into my memory never to die.

One night I remember being stopped by a sentry at "Dead Man's Curve," because the Boche was shelling the curve that night, and we had to stop until he "laid off," as the sentry told us. Between shells there was a great stillness on the white road that lay like a silver thread under the moonlight. The shattered stone buildings, with a great cathedral tower standing like a gaunt ghost above the ruins, were tragically beautiful under that mellow light. One almost forgot there was war under the charm of that scene until "plunk! plunk! plunk!" the big shells fell from time to time. But the thing that impressed me most that waiting hour was not the beauty of the village under the moonlight, but the fact that the lone sentry who had stopped us, and who amid the shelling stood silently, was unconsciously singing an old hymn of the church, "Rock of Ages, Cleft for Me." I got down from my truck and walked over to where he was standing.

"Great old hymn, isn't it, lad?"

"I'll say so," was his laconic reply.

"Belong to some church back home?" I asked him.

"Folks do; Presbyterians," he replied.

"Like the old hymns?" I asked.

"Yes, it seems like home to sing 'em."

I didn't get to talk with him for a few minutes, for he had to stop another truck. Then he came back.

"Folks at home, Sis and Bill and the kid, mother and father, used to gather around the piano every Sunday evening and sing 'em. Didn't think much of them then, but liked to sing. But they mean a lot to me over here, especially when I'm on guard at nights on this 'Dead Man's Curve.' Seems like they make me stronger." As I walked away I still heard him humming "Rock of Ages, Cleft for Me."

One of the most vivid song silhouettes that I remember is that of a great crowd of negroes singing in a Y. M. C. A. hut. There must have been a thousand of them. I was to speak to them on "Lincoln Day." I remember how their white teeth shone through the semidarkness of that candle-lighted hut, and how their eyes gleamed, and how their bodies swayed as they sang the old plantation melodies.

The first song startled me with the universality of its simple expression. It was an adaptation of that old melody which the negroes have sung for years, "It's the Old-Time Religion."

A boy down front led the singing. A curt "Sam, set up a tune," from the Tuskegee colored secretary started it.

This boy sat with his back to the audience. He didn't even turn around to face them. Low and sweetly he started singing. You could hardly hear him at first. Then a few boys near him took up the music. Then a few more. Then it gradually swept back over that crowd of men until every single negro was swaying to that simple music, and then it was that I caught the almost startlingly appropriate words:

"It is good for a world in trouble;
It is good for a world in trouble;
It is good for a world in trouble;
    And it's good enough for me.

It's the old-time religion;
It's the old-time religion;
It's the old-time religion;
    And it's good enough for me.

It was good for my old mother;
It was good for my old mother;
It was good for my old mother;
    And it's good enough for me."

Then much to my astonishment they did something that I have since learned is the very way that these songs grew from the beginning. They extemporized a verse for the day, and they did it on the spot. I made absolutely certain of that by careful investigation. They sang this extra verse:

"It was good for ole Abe Lincoln;
It was good for ole Abe Lincoln;
It was good for ole Abe Lincoln;
    And it's good enough for me."

"That first verse, 'It is good for a world in trouble,' is certainly a most appropriate one for these times in France," I said aside to the secretary.

"Yes," he replied; "if ever this pore ole worl' needed the sustainin' power of the religion of the Christ, it does now; an' if ever this pore ole worl' was in trouble, that time suttinly is right now," he added with fervor.

And now I can never think of the world, nor of the folks back here at home, nor of the millions of our boys over there that I do not hear the sweet voices of that crowd of negroes singing reverently and fervently:

"It is good for a world in trouble;
It is good for a world in trouble;
It is good for a world in trouble;
And it's good enough for me."

Another Silhouette of Song that stands out against the background of memory is that of a hymn that I heard in Doctor Charles Jefferson's church just before I sailed for France. I was lonely. I walked into that great city church a stranger, as thousands of boys who have sailed from New York have done. I never remember to have been so unutterably lonely and homesick. It was cold in the city, and I was alone. I turned to a church. Thousands of boys have done the same, may the mothers and fathers of America know, and they have found comfort. If the parents of this great nation could know how well their boys are guarded and cared for in New York City before they sail, they would have a feeling of comfort.

I sat down in this great church. I was thinking more of other Sabbath mornings at home, with my wife and baby, than anything else. A hymn was announced. I stood up mechanically, but there was no song in my throat. There was a great lump of loneliness only. But suddenly I listened to the words they were singing. Had they selected that hymn just for me? It seemed so. It so answered the loneliness in my heart with comfort and quiet. That great congregation was singing:

"Peace, perfect peace;
With loved ones far away;
In Jesus' keeping, we are safe; and they."

A great sense of peace settled over my heart, and I have quoted that old hymn all over France to the boys, and they have been comforted. Many a boy has asked me to write him a copy of that verse to stick in his notebook. It seemed to give a sense of comfort to the lads, for their loved ones, too, were "far away," and since I have come home I find that this, too, comes as a great comfort hymn to those who are here lonely for their boys "over there."

And who shall forget the silhouette of approaching the shores of France by night as they have sailed down along the coast, cautiously and carefully, to find the opening of the submarine nets? Who shall forget the sense of exhilaration that the news that land was near brought? Who shall forget the crowding to the railings by all on board to scan anxiously through the night for the first sight of land? Then who shall forget seeing that first light from shore flash out through the darkness of night? Who shall forget the red and green and white lights that began to twinkle, and gleam, and flash, and signal, and call? How beautiful those lights looked after the long, dangerous, eventful, and dark voyage, without a single light showing on the ship! And who shall forget the man along the railing who said, "I never knew before the meaning of that old song, 'The Lights Along the Shore'"? And then, who can forget the fact that suddenly somebody started to sing that old hymn, "The Lights Along the Shore," and of how it swept along the lower decks, and then to the upper decks, until a whole ship-load of people was singing it? And then who shall forget how somebody else started "Let the Lower Lights Be Burning"? Can such scenes ever be obliterated from one's memory? No, not forever. That silhouette remains eternally!

Five great transports were in. They were lined up along the docks in the locks. A Y. M. C. A. secretary was standing on the docks yelling up a word of welcome to the crowded railings of the great transports. The boats were not "cleared" as yet. It would take an hour, and the secretary knew that something must be done, so he started to lead first one ship and then another in singing.

"What shall we sing, boys?" he would shout up to them from the docks below. Some fellow from the railing yelled, "Keep the Home Fires Burning," and that fine song rang out from five thousand throats. I have heard it sung in the camps at home, I have heard it sung in great huts in France, but I never heard it when it sounded so significant and so sweet in its mighty volume as it sounded coming from that great khaki-lined transport, which had just landed an hour before in France. I stood beside the song-leader there on the docks looking up at that great mass of American humanity, a hundred feet above us, so far away that we could not recognize individual faces, on the high decks of one of the largest ships that sails the seas, and as that sweet song of war swept out over the docks and across the white town, and back across the Atlantic, I said to myself: "That volume sounds as if it could make itself heard back home."

The man beside me said: "The folks back home hear it all right, for they are eagerly listening for every sound that comes from that crowd of boys. Yes, the folks back home hear it, and they'll 'keep the home fires burning' all right. God bless them!"

The last Silhouette of Song stands out against a background of green trees and spring, and the odor of a hospital, and Red Cross nurses going and coming, and boys lying in white robes everywhere. My friend the song-leader had gone with me to hold the vesper service in the hospital. Then we visited in the wards in order to see those who were so severely wounded that they could not get to the service.

There was a little group of men in one room. The first thing I knew my friend had them singing. At first they took to it awkwardly. Then more courageously. Then sweetly there rang through the hospital the strains of "My Daddy Over There."

It melted my heart, for I have a baby girl at home who says to the neighbors, "My daddy is the prettiest man in the world," and believes it. I said to Cray: "Why did you sing that particular song?"

"Oh," he replied, "my baby's name is 'Betty,' and I found a guy whose baby's name is 'Betty' too, and we had a sort of club formed; and another guy had a baby boy, and then I just thought they'd like to sing 'My Daddy Over There.' But we ended up with 'Jesus, Lover of My Soul,' so that ought to suit you."

"Suit me, man? Why I got a 'Betty' baby of my own, and that 'Daddy Over There' song you sang is the sweetest thing I've heard in France, and it will help those daddies more than a hymn would. I'm glad you got them to singing."

And now I'm back home, and I thought the Silhouettes of Song were all over, but I stepped into a church the other Sunday. Up high above the sacred altars of that church fluttered a beautiful silk service flag. It was starred in the shape of a letter "S." In the circle of each "S" was a red cross. The church had two members in the Red Cross. Above the "S" and below it were two red triangles. The church had men in the service of the Y. M. C. A. Then grouped about the "S" were the stars of boys in the service.

As I looked up at this cross a flood of memories swept over me. I could not keep back the tears. All the love, all the loneliness, all the heartache, all the pride, all the hope of the folks at home, their reverence, their loyalty, was summed up in that flag. I stood to sing, my eyes brimming with tears. The great congregation started that beautifully sweet hymn that is being sung all over America in the churches in loving memory of the boys over there:

"God save our splendid men,
Send them safe home again,
    God save our men.
Make them victorious,
Patient and chivalrous,

They are so dear to us,
        God save our men.

God keep our own dear men,
From every stain of sin,
        God keep our men.
When Satan would allure,
When tempted, keep them pure,
Be their protection sure—
        God keep our men.

God hold our precious men,
And love them to the end.
        God hold our men.
Held in Thine arms so strong
To Thee they all belong.
This ever be our song:
        God hold our men."

I stood the pressure until that great congregation came to that line "They are so dear to us," and the voice of the mother beside me broke, and she had to stop. Then I had to stop, too, and we looked at each other through our tears and smiled and understood, so that when she sweetly said, "I have a boy over there," her words were superfluous. And so I have added another memory of song to the hours that will never die.

II
SHIP SILHOUETTES

It was nearing the dawn, and flaming heralds gave promise of a brilliant day coming up out of France to the east. Three of us stood in the "crow's-nest" on an American transport, where we had been standing our "watch" since four o'clock that morning.

Suddenly as we peered through our glasses off to the west we saw the masts of a great cruiser creeping above the horizon of the sea. We reported it to the "bridge," where it was confirmed. Then in a few minutes we saw another mast, and then another, and another; four, five, six, seven, eight, nine, ten, twenty—five, six—twenty-six ships coming up over the western horizon, bound for France, bearing the most precious burden that ever a caravan of the sea carried across the waters of the deep; American boys! Your boys!

It was a marvellous sight. We had been so intently watching this that we had forgotten about the dawn. Then we turned for a minute, and off to the east a brilliant red dawn was splashing its way out of the sea.

"What are those dots on the sun?" Doctor Freeman shouted to me.

[Illustration: "What are those dots on the sun?" Doctor Freeman shouted to me.]

"Why, I believe it's the convoy of destroyers coming out to meet those transports," I replied.

Then before our eyes, up out of the eastern horizon, just as we had watched the transports and the cruiser come up over the western horizon, those slender guardians of the deep came toward us in formation. There were ten of them, and they met the great American convoy just abreast our transport. We saw the American flag fly to the winds on each ship, and the flashing of signal-lights even in the dawning.

"Those destroyers coming out of the east against that sunrise remind me of the experiences one has in France in these vivid war days," I said to my fellow watcher in the "crow's-nest."

"How is that?"

"They stand out like the Silhouettes of Mountain Peaks against a crimson sunrise," I replied.

And so have many Silhouettes of the Sea stood out.

There was the afternoon that we stood on the deck of a ship bound for France. The voyage had been full of dangers. Submarines had harassed us for days. One night such a lurch came to the ship as threw everybody about in their staterooms. We thought it was a storm until the morning came, and we were informed that it was a sudden lurch to avoid a submarine. The voyage had been full of uneasiness, and now we were coming to the most dangerous part of it, the submarine zone.

Everybody was on deck. It was Sunday afternoon. Suddenly off to the east several spots appeared on the horizon. What were they, friendly craft or enemy ships?

Nobody knew, not even the captain. There was a wave of uneasiness over the boat.

Speculation was rife.

Then we saw the signal boy go aft, and in a moment the tricolor of France was fluttering in the winds, and we knew that the approaching craft were friendly. Then through powerful glasses we could make them out to be long, low-lying, lithe, swift destroyers coming out to meet us. They were a welcome sight. Like "hounds of the sea" they came, long and lean. Headed straight for us, they came like the winds. Then suddenly a slight mist began to fall, but not enough to obscure either the destroyers or the sun. Through this mist the sun burned its way, and almost as if a miracle had been performed by some master artist, a beautiful rainbow arched the sky to the east, and under the arch of this rainbow fleetly sailed those approaching destroyers.

It was a beautiful sight, a Silhouette of the Sea never to be forgotten while memory lasts. The French flag fluttered, the band started to play the "Marseillaise," and a ship-load of happy people sang it.

A sense of peace settled down over us all. The rainbow, covenant of old, promise of the eternal God to his people, seemed to have new significance that memorable day.

Another Silhouette of the Sea! Troops are expected in at a certain port of entry. The camp has been emptied of ten thousand men. That means but one thing, that new troops are expected. The great dirigibles sailed out a few hours ago. The sea-planes followed. Thousands of American men and women lined the docks waiting, peering with anxious eyes out toward the "point." Here at this point a great cape jutted out into the ocean, and around this cape we were accustomed to catch sight of the convoys first.

A sense of great expectancy was upon us. We had heard rumors of submarines off the shore for several days. Then suddenly we heard a terrific cannonading, and we knew that the transports and the convoys were in a battle with the U-boats that had lain in wait for them. An anxious hour passed. The sun was setting and the west was a great rose blanket.

Then a shout went up far down the line of waiting Americans as the first great transport swung around the cape. Then another, and a third and a fourth, and finally a fifth; great gray bulks, two of them camouflaged until you could not tell whether they were little destroyers or a group of destroyers on one big ship. Then they got near enough to see the American boys, thousands of them, lining the railings. Through the glasses we could make out the names of the transports. They were some of the largest that sail the Atlantic. When as they came slowly in on the full tide, with that rose sunset back of them, the bands on their decks playing across the waters, and five thousand boys on the first boat singing "Keep the Home Fires Burning," then the "Marseillaise," and finally "The Star-Spangled Banner," in which the crowd on the shore joined, there was a Silhouette of the Sea that burned its way into our souls.

There were the great ships, and beyond them the cape, and beyond that the hovering dirigibles, and beyond them the great bird seaplanes, and beyond them the background of a rose-colored sky, and beyond that the memories of home.

III
SILHOUETTES OF SACRIFICE

Every day for two months, February and March, sometimes when the roads were hub-deep with mud, and sometimes when the roads were a glare of ice and snow and driving the big truck was dangerous work, we passed the crucifix.

It was the guide-post where four roads forked. One road went up to the old monastery, where we had, in one corner, a canteen. Another road led down toward divisional headquarters. Another road led into Toul, and a fourth led directly toward the German lines, over which, if we had driven far enough, as we started to do one night in the dark, we could have gone straight to Berlin.

The first night that I went "down the line" alone with a truck-load I was trembling inside about directions. The divisional man said: "Go straight out the east gate of the city, down the road until you come to the cross at the forks of the road. Take the turn to the left."

But even with these directions I was not certain. I was frankly afraid, for I knew that a wrong turn would take me into German lines. I did not like that prospect at all.

I drove the big car cautiously through the night. There were no lights, and at best it was not easy driving. This night was impenetrably dark. When I came to the cross-roads I stopped the machine and climbed down. I wanted to make sure of the directions, and they were printed in French on the sign-board that was near the crucifix about which he had told me.

I got my directions all right, and then, moved by curiosity, flashed my pocket-light on the figure of the bronze Christ on the crucifix there at the crossroads guide-post. There was an inscription. Laboriously finding each small letter with my flash in the darkness, my engine panting off to the side of the road, I spelled it all out:

"Traveller, hast thou ever seen so great a grief as mine?"

Off in the near distance the star-shells were lighting up No Man's Land. "Traveller, hast thou ever seen so great a grief as mine?" they seemed to say to me.

I climbed into the machine and started on.

Suddenly I heard the purring of Boche planes overhead. One gets so that he can distinguish the difference between French planes and Boche planes. These were Boche planes, and they were bent on mischief. Then the search-lights began to play in the sky over me. But they were too late, for hardly had I started on my way when "Boom! boom! boom! boom!" one after another, ten bombs were dropped, and as each dropped it lighted up the surrounding country like a great city in flames.

As I saw this awful desecration of the land the phrase of the cross seemed to sing in unison with the beating of the engine of my truck:

"Traveller, hast thou ever seen so great a grief as mine?"

Suddenly out of the night crept an ambulance train, which passed my slower and larger machine. They had no time to wait for me. They were American boys on their errands of mercy, and the front was calling them. I knew that something must be going on off toward the front lines, for the rumbling of the big guns had been going on for an hour. As these ambulances passed me—more than twenty-five of them passed as silent ships pass in the night—that phrase kept singing: "Traveller, hast thou ever seen so great a grief as mine?"

Then I drove a bit farther on my way, and off across a field I saw the walls of a great hospital. It was an evacuation hospital, and I had visited in its wards many times after a raid, when hundreds of our boys had been brought in every night and day, with four shifts of doctors kept busy day and night in the operating-room caring for them. As I thought of all that I had seen in that hospital, again that singing phrase of the crucifix at the crossroads was on my lips: "Traveller, hast thou ever seen so great a grief as mine?"

A mile farther, and just a few feet from the road, I passed a little "God's acre" that I knew so well. As its full meaning swept over me there in the darkness of that night, the heartache and loneliness of the folks at home whose American boys were lying there, some two hundred of them, the old crucifix phrase expressed it all:

"Traveller, hast thou ever seen so great a grief as mine?"

And, somehow, as I drove back by the crucifix in the darkness of the next morning, about two o'clock, I had to stop again and with my flash-light spell out the lettering on the cross.

Then suddenly it dawned on me that this was France speaking to America:

"Traveller, hast thou ever seen so great a grief as mine?"

And when I paused in the darkness of that night and thought of the one million and a quarter of the best manhood of France who had given their lives for the precious things that we hold most dear: our homes, our children, our liberty, our democracy; and when I thought that France had saved that for us; and when I remembered the funeral processions that I had seen every day since I had been in France, and when I remembered the women doing the work of men, handling the baggage of France, ploughing the fields of France; doing the work of men because the men were all either killed or at the front; when I remembered the little fatherless children that I had seen all over France, whose sad eyes looked up into mine everywhere I went; and when I remembered the young widows (every woman of France seems to be in black); and when I remembered the thousands of blind men and boys that I had seen being led helplessly about the streets of the cities and villages of France; and when I remembered that lonely wife that one Sunday afternoon in Toul I had watched go and kneel beside a little mound and place flowers there—the dates on the stone of which I later saw were "March, 1916," then I cried aloud in the darkness as I realized the tremendous sacrifice that France has made for the world, as well as England and Belgium. "No, France! No, England! No, little Belgium! this traveller has never seen so great a grief as thine!"

"No, mothers and fathers, little children, wives, brothers, sisters of France, and England, and Belgium, this traveller, America, has never seen so great a grief as thine!"

And later I learned, after living in the Toul sector for two months, that the challenging sentence on the crucifix had been read by nearly every boy who had passed it; and all had. Either he had read it himself or it had been quoted to him, and this one crucifix question had much to do with challenging the boys who passed it to a new understanding of all that France had passed through in the war.

The American boys have learned to respect the French soldier because of the sacrifice that he has made. The American soldier remembers that crowd of men called "Kitchener's Mob," which Kitchener sent into the trenches of France to stem the tide of inhumanity, and to whom he gave a message: "Go! Sacrifice yourselves while I raise an army in England!" The American soldier knows all of this. He knows that little Belgium might have said to all the world, "The forces were too great for us," and she could have stepped aside and the world would have forgiven her.

But instead she chose deliberately to sacrifice herself for the cause of freedom, and sacrifice herself she did. And that sentence on the crossroads crucifix in the Toul sector, day after day, sends its reminder into the heart of the American soldiers, who stop their trucks and their ammunition wagons, pause their weary marches to read it; sends its reminder of the sacrifices that our allies have already made, and the sacrifices that we may be called upon to make. "Traveller, hast thou ever seen so great a grief as mine?"

And the American officer and soldier must admit that he has not; and he prays God silently in the night as he rides by on his horse, or as he drives by on his motor-truck, or as he flashes by on his motor-cycle, though they may be willing to suffer as France has suffered, if need be, prays God that that may never be necessary, for the American soldier, since he has been in France, has seen what suffering means.

And so that crossroads crucifix stands out against the lurid night of France, with its reminder constantly before the American soldier, and it tends to make him more gentle with French children and women, and more kindly with French men. There is a new understanding of each other, a new cement of friendship binding our allies together in France; there is a new world-wide brotherhood breaking across the horizon of time, coming through sacrifice.

The world is once again being atoned for. Its sin is being washed away. Innocent men are suffering that humanity may be saved.

The last time I saw this cross was by night. I had seen it first at night, and fitting it was that I should see it last at night. There was a terrible bombardment down the lines. Hundreds of American boys had been killed. One was wounded who was a son of one of the foremost Americans. News of the fight had been coming in to us all day long. Night came and "runners" were still bringing in the gruesome details. The ambulances were running in a continuous procession. We had seen things that day and night that made our hearts sick. We had seen American boys white and unconscious. We had seen every available room in the great evacuation hospital crowded. We had been told that a hundred surgical cases were in the hospital, mostly shrapnel wounds, and that every available doctor and nurse was working night and day.

We had seen, under one snow-covered canvas, six boys who had been killed by one shell early that morning—boys that the night before we had talked with down in a front-line hut—boys who had been killed in their billet in one room. We had seen a captain come staggering into our hut wet to the skin, soaked with blood, his hair dishevelled, his face haggard. He had been fighting since three o'clock that morning. He had been shell-shocked, and had been sent into the hospital.

"My God!" he cried, "I saw every officer in my company killed. First it was my first lieutenant. They got him in the head. Then about ten o'clock

I saw my second lieutenant fall. Then early in the afternoon my top-sergeant got a bayonet, and a hand-grenade got a group of my non-commissioned officers. Half of my boys are gone."

Then he sat down and we got him some hot chocolate. This seemed to revive his spirits, and he said: "But, thank God, we licked them! We licked them at their own game! We got them six to one, and drove them back! No Man's Land is thick with their beastly bodies. They are hanging on the wires out there like trapped rabbits!"

Then the thoughts of his own officers came back.

"My God! Now we know what war means. We've been playing at war up to this time. Now we've got to suffer! Then we'll know what it all means." He was half-delirious, we could see, and sent for an ambulance.

As I drove home that night I passed the crossroads crucifix. This time I needed no lights to guide me. The whole horizon was alight with bursting shells and Very lights. Long before I got to it I could see the gaunt form of the cross reaching its black but comforting arms up against the background of lurid light along the front where I knew that American men were dying for me. The picture of that wayside cross, looming against the lurid light of battle, shall never die in my memory.

It was the silhouette of France and America suffering together, a silhouette standing out against a livid horizon of fire.

I needed no tiny pocket search-light to read the words on the cross. They had already burned their way into my heart and into the hearts of that whole division of American soldiers, that division which has since so distinguished itself at Belleau Woods! But now America has a new understanding of the meaning of that sentence, for America, too, is suffering, and she is sacrificing.

"Traveller, hast thou ever seen so great a grief as mine?"

"Yes, France; we understand now."

IV
SILHOUETTES SPIRITUAL

It was the gas ward. I had held a vesper service that evening and had had a strange experience. Just before the service I had been introduced to a lad who said to the chaplain who introduced me that he was a member of my denomination.

The boy could not speak above a whisper. He was gassed horribly, and in addition to his lungs being burned out and his throat, his face and neck were scarred.

"I have as many scars on my lungs as I have on my face," he said quite simply. I had to bend close to hear him. He could not talk loud enough to have awakened a sleeping child.

He said to me: "I used to be leader of the choir at home. At college I was in the glee-club, and whenever we had any singin' at the fraternity house they always expected me to lead it. Since I came into the army the boys in my outfit have depended upon me for all the music. In camp back home I led the singing. Even the Y. M. C. A. always counted on me to lead the singing in the religious meetings. Many's the time I have cheered the boys comin' over on the transport and in camp by singin' when they were blue. But I can't sing any more. Sometimes I get pretty blue over that. But I'll be at your meeting this evening, anyway, and I'll be right down on the front seat as near the piano as I can get. Watch for me."

And sure enough that night, when the vesper service started, he was right there. I smiled at him and he smiled back.

I announced the first hymn. The crowd started to sing. Suddenly I looked toward him. We were singing "Softly Now the Light of Day Fades Upon My Sight Away." His book was up, his lips were moving, but no sound was coming. That sight nearly broke my heart. To see that boy, whose whole passion in the past had been to sing, whose voice the cruel gas had burned out, started emotions throbbing in me that blurred my eyes. I couldn't sing another note myself. My voice was choked at the sight. A lump came every time I looked at him there with that book up in front of him, a lump that I could not get out of my throat. I dared not look in his direction.

After the service was over I went up to him. I knew that he needed a bit of laughter now. I knew that I did, too. So I said to him: "Lad, I don't know what I would have done if you hadn't helped us out on the singing this evening."

He looked at me with infinite pathos and sorrow in his eyes. Then a look of triumph came into them, and he looked up and whispered through his rasped voice: "I may not be able to make much noise any more, and I may never be able to lead the choir again, but I'll always have singing in my soul, sir! I'll always have singing in my soul!"

And so it is with the whole American army in France—it always has singing in its soul, and courage, and manliness, and daring, and hope. That kind of an army can never be defeated. And no army in the world, and no power, can stand long before that kind of an army.

That kind of an army doesn't have to be sent into battle with a barrage of shells in front of it and a barrage of shells back of it to force it in, as the Germans have been doing during the last big offensive, according to stories that boys at Château-Thierry have been telling me. The kind of an army that, in spite of wounds and gas, "still has singing in its soul" will conquer all hell on earth before it gets through.

Then there is the memory of the boys in the shell-shock ward at this same hospital. I had a long visit with them. They were not permitted to come to the vesper service for fear something would happen to upset their nerves. But they made a special request that I come to visit them in their ward. After the service I went. I reached their ward about nine, and they arose to greet me. The nurse told me that they were more at ease on their feet than lying down, and so for two hours we stood and talked on our feet.

"How did you get yours?" I asked a little black-eyed New Yorker.

"I was in a front-line trench with my 'outfit,' down near Amiens," he said. "We were having a pretty warm scrap. I was firing a machine-gun so fast that it was red-hot. I was afraid it would melt down, and I would be up against it. They were coming over in droves, and we were mowing them down so fast that out in front of our company they looked like stacks of hay, the dead Germans piled up everywhere. I was so busy firing my gun, and watching it so carefully because it was so hot, that I didn't hear the shell that suddenly burst behind me. If I had heard it coming it would never have shocked me."

"If you hear them coming you're all right?" I asked.

"Yes. It's the ones that surprise you that give you shell-shock. If you hear the whine you're ready for them; but if your mind is on something else, as mine was that day, and the thing bursts close, it either kills you or gives you shell-shock, so it gets you both going and coming." He laughed at this.

"I was all right for a while after the thing fell, for I was unconscious for a half-hour. When I came to I began to shake, and I've been shaking ever since."

"How did you get yours?" I asked another lad, from Kansas, for I saw at once that it eased them to talk about it.

"I was in a trench when a big Jack Johnson burst right behind me. It killed six of the boys, all my friends, and buried me under the dirt that fell from the parapet back of me. I had sense and strength enough to dig myself out. When I got out I was kind of dazed. The captain told me to go back to the rear. I started back through the communication-trench and got lost. The next thing I knew I was wandering around in the darkness shakin' like a leaf."

Then there was the California boy. I had known him before. It was he who almost gave me a case of shell-shock. The last time I saw him he was standing on a platform addressing a crowd of young church people in California. And there he was, his six foot three shaking from head to foot like an old man with palsy, and stuttering every word he spoke. He had been sent to the hospital at Amiens with a case of acute appendicitis. The first night he was in the hospital the Germans bombed it and destroyed it. They took him out and put him on a train for Paris. This train had only gotten a few miles out of Amiens when the Germans shelled it and destroyed two cars.

"After that I began to shake," he said simply.

"No wonder, man; who wouldn't shake after that?" I said. Then I asked him if he had had his operation yet.

"It can't be done until I quit shaking."

"When will you quit?" I asked, with a smile.

"Oh, we're all getting better, much better; we'll be out of here in a few months; they all get better; 90 per cent of us get back in the trenches."

And that is the silver lining to this Silhouette Spiritual. The doctors say that a very large percentage of them get back.

"We call ourselves the 'First American Shock Troops,'" my friend from the West said with a grin.

"I guess you are 'shock troops,' all right. I know one thing, and that is that you would give your folks back home a good shock if they saw you."

Then we all laughed. Laughter was in the air. I have never met anywhere in France such a happy, hopeful, cheerful crowd as that bunch of shell-shocked boys. It was contagious. I went there to cheer them up, and I got cheered up. I went there to give them strength, and came away stronger than when I went in. It would cheer the hearts of all Americans to take a peep into that room; if they could see the souls back of the trembling bodies; if they could get beyond the first shock of those trembling bodies and stuttering tongues. And, after all, that is what America must learn to do, to get beyond, and to see beyond, the wounds, into the soul of the boy; to see beyond the blinded eyes, the scarred faces, the legless and armless lads, into the glory of their new-born souls, for no boy goes through the hell of fire and suffering and wounds that he does not come out new-born. The old man is gone from him, and a new man is born in him. That is the great eternal compensation of war and suffering.

I have seen boys come out of battles made new men. I have seen them go into the line sixteen-year-old lads, and come out of the trenches men. I saw a lad who had gone through the fighting in Belleau Woods. I talked with him in the hospital at Paris. His face was terribly wounded. He was ugly to look at, but when I talked with him I found a soul as white as a lily and as courageous as granite.

"I may look awful," he said, "but I'm a new man inside. What I saw out there in the woods made me different, somehow. I saw a friend stand by his machine-gun, with a whole platoon of Germans sweeping down on him, and he never flinched. He fired that old gun until every bullet was gone and his gun was red-hot. I was lying in the grass where I could see it all. I saw them bayonet him. He fought to the last against fifty men, but, thank God, he died a man; he died an American. I lay there and cried to see them kill him, but every time I think of that fellow it makes me want to be more of a man. When I get back home I'm going to give up my life to some kind of Christian service. I'm going to do it because I saw that man die so bravely. If he can die like that, in spite of my face I can live like a man."

The boys in the trenches live a year in a month, a month in a week, a week in a day, a day in an hour, and sometimes an eternity in a second. No wonder it makes men of them overnight. No wonder they come out of it all with that "high look" that John Oxenham writes about. They have been reborn.

Another wounded boy who had gone through the fighting back of Montdidier said to me in the hospital:

"I never thought of anybody else at home but myself. I was selfish. Sis and mother did everything for me. Everything at home centred in me, and everything was arranged for my comfort. With this leg gone I might have some right now, according to the way they think, to that attention, but I don't want it any longer. I can't bear the thoughts of having people do for me. I want to spend the rest of my life doing things for other folks.

"Back of Noyon I saw a friend sail into a crowd of six Germans with nothing but his bayonet and rifle. They had surrounded his captain, and were rushing him back as a prisoner. They evidently had orders to take the officers alive as prisoners. That big top-sergeant sailed into them, and after killing two of them, knocking two more down, and giving his captain a chance to escape, the last German shot him through the head. He gave his life for the captain. That has changed me. I shall never be the same again after seeing that happen. There's something come into my heart. I'm going back home a Christian man."

Yes, America must learn to see beyond the darkness, beyond the disfigured face, to the soul of the boy. And America will do it. America is like that. And so back of these shaking bodies and these stuttering tongues of the shell-shocked boys I saw their wonderful souls. And after spending that two hours with them I can never be the same man again.

I could, as Donald Hankey says, "get down on my knees and shine their boots for them any day," and thank God for the privilege. I think that this is the spirit of any non-combatant in France who has any immediate contact with our men on the battle-front or in the hospitals. They are so brave and so true.

"How do the Americans stand dressing their wounds and the suffering in the hospitals?" a friend of mine asked a prominent surgeon.

"They bear their suffering like Frenchmen. That is the highest compliment I can pay them," he replied.

And so back of their wounds are their immortal, undying, unflinching souls. And back of the tremblings of these boys that night, thank God, I had the glory of seeing their immortal souls, and to me the soul of an American boy under fire and pain is the biggest, finest, most tremendous thing on earth. I bow before it in humility. It dazzled mine eyes. All I could think of as I saw it was:

"Mine eyes have seen the glory of the coming of the Lord."

That night I said, just before I left: "Boys, it's Sunday evening, and they wouldn't let you come to my meeting! Would you like for me to have a little prayer with you?"

"Yes! Sure! That's just what we want!" were the stammered words that followed.

"All right; we'll just stand, if it's easier for you."

Then I prayed the prayer that had been burning in my heart every minute as we stood there in that dimly lit ward, talking of home and battle and the folks we all loved across the seas. All that time there had been hovering in the background of my mind a picture of a cool body of water named Galilee, and of a Christ who had been sleeping in a boat on that water with some of his friends, when a storm came up. I had been thinking of how frightened those friends had been of the storm; of the tossing, tumbling, turbulent waves. I had thought of how they had trembled with fear, and then of how they had appealed to the Master. I told the boys simply that story, and then I prayed:

"O Thou Christ who stilled the waves of Galilee, come Thou into the hearts of these boys just now, and still their trembling limbs and tongues. Bring a great sense of peace and quiet into their souls."

"Oh, ye of little faith!" When I looked up from that prayer, much to my own astonishment, and to the astonishment of the friend who was with me, the tremblings of those fine American boys had perceptibly ceased. There was a great sense of quiet and peace in the ward.

The nurse told me the next day that after I had gone the boys went quietly to bed; that there was little tossing that night and no walking the floors, as there had been before. A doctor friend said to me: "After all, maybe your medicine is best, for while we are more or less groping in the dark as to our treatment of shell-shock, we do know that the only cure will be that something comes into their souls to give them quiet of mind and peace within."

"I know what that medicine is," I told him. "I have seen it work."

"What is it?" he asked.

Then I told him of my experience.

"You may be right."

And so it is all over France; where I have worked in some twenty hospitals—from the first-aid dressing-stations back through the evacuation hospitals to the base hospitals—and have found that the reaction of our boys to wounds and suffering is always a spiritual reaction. I know as I know no other thing, that the boys of America are to come back, wounded or otherwise, a better crowd of men than they went away. They are men reborn, and when they come back, when it's "over, over there," there is to be a nation reborn because of the leaven that is within their souls.

V
SILHOUETTES OF SACRILEGE

During the last year there has come into French art a new era of the silhouette. In every art store in Paris one sees wonderful silhouettes which tell the story of the horror of the Hun better than any words can paint it, and when one attempts to paint it he must attempt it in word silhouettes.

The silhouette catches the picture better than color. Gaunt, naked, ruined cathedrals, homes, towers, and forests are better pictured in black silhouettes than any other way. There is nothing much left in some places in France but silhouettes.

Those who have seen Rheims know that the best reproduction of its ruins has been conveyed by the simple silhouette of the artist. There it stands outlined against the sky. Rheims that was once the wonder of the world is now naked ruins, tottering walls, with its towers still standing, looming against the sky like tottering trees. And when, during the past year, the walls fell, they:

"Left a lonesome place against the sky"

of all the world.

The church at Albert was like that. Only a silhouette can describe or picture it. There it stood against the sky by day and night, with the figure on its top leaning. The old legend of the soldiers that when the figure of the Virgin fell to the earth the war would end has been dissipated, for during the last drive that figure fell, and the tower with it. But forever (although it has fallen to dust and debris, because of descriptions we have seen of it) it shall stand out in our memories like a lonely, toppling tree against a crimson sunset!

Every day on the Toul line we used to drive through a village that had been shelled until it was in ruins. Only the tower and the walls of a beautiful little church remained. Every other house in the village was razed to the ground. Nothing else remained.

There it stands to this day, for when I saw it last in June it was still standing as it was in January. Every evening about sunset we used to drive down that way, taking supplies to the front-line huts. Many things stand out in one's memory of a certain road over which he drives night after night and day after day. There is the cross at the forks of the roads. There is the old monastery, battered and in ruins, that stood out like a gaunt ghost of the vandal Hun. There was the little God's acre along the road which we passed every day. There were always the observation-balloons against the evening sky. There were always the fleet-winged birds of the air outlined against the evening. There were always the marching men and the ambulance trains. But standing out above them all, etched with the acid of regret and anger and horror, stood that lonely tower. Night after night we approached it with a beautiful sunset off to the west where the Germans lay buried in their trenches. Coming back from the German lines we would see this church-tower outlined against the crimson sky like a finger pointing God-ward, and declaring to all the world that the God above would avenge this silent, accusing Silhouette of Sacrilege.

There has been a good deal of discussion over a certain book entitled "I Accuse." I never saw that finger pointing into the sky as we drove through this village that it did not cry out to the heavens and across the short miles to the German Huns, looking down, as it did, at its feet where the ruined homes lay, the village that it had mothered and fathered, the village that had worshipped within its simple walls, the village that had brought its joys and sorrows there, the village that had buried the dead within its shadows, the village that had brought its young there to be married and its aged to be buried; there it stood, night after night, against the crimson sky sometimes, against the golden sky at other times; against the rose, against the blue, against the purple sunsets; and ever it thundered: "I accuse! I accuse! I accuse!"

Then there is that Silhouette of Sacrilege up on the Baupaume Road. This is called "the saddest road in Christendom," because more men have been killed along its scarred pathway than along any other road in all the world. Not even the road to Calvary was as sad as this road.

Along this road when the French held it, during the first year of the war, they gathered their dead together and buried them in a little cemetery. Above the sacred remains of their comrades these French soldiers erected a simple bronze cross as a symbol not only of the faith of the nation, but a symbol also of the cause in which they had died.

A few months later when the Germans had recaptured this spot, and it had been fought over, and the bronze cross still stood, the Hun, too, gathered his dead together and buried them side by side with the French. Then he did a characteristic thing. He got a large stone as a base and mounted a cannon-ball on top of this stone, and left it there, side by side with the French cross.

Whether he meant it or not, his sacrilege stands as a fitting expression of his philosophy, the philosophy of the brute, the religion of the granite rock and the iron cannon-ball.

He told his own story here. Side by side in those two monuments the contrast is made, the causes are placed. One is the cause of the cross, the cause of men willing to die for brotherhood; the other is the cause of those who are willing to kill to conquer.

And these two monuments, side by side on the Baupaume Road, stand out as one of the Silhouettes of Sacrilege.

Then there is St. Gervais. On Good Friday afternoon a Hun shell pierced the side of this beautiful cathedral as the spear-thrust pierced the side of the Master so long ago. On the very hour that Jesus was crucified back on that other and first Good Friday the Hun threw his bolt of death into the nave of this church, and crucified seventy-five people kneeling in memory of their Saviour's death.

I was in that church an hour after this terrible sacrilege happened. Never can one forget the scene. I dare not describe it here in its awful details.

The entire arches of stone that held up the roof had fallen in from the concussion of the gases of the shell. Three feet of solid stones covered the floor. Men and women were being carried out. Silk hats, canes, shoes, hats, baby clothes, an expensive fur, lay buried in the stone and dirt.

As I stood horrified, looking on this scene of death and destruction, the phrase came into my heart:

"And the veil of the temple was rent in twain."

And this scene, too, shall remain as one of the Silhouettes of Sacrilege.

But perhaps the worst Silhouette of Sacrilege that the film of one's memory has brought away from France is that of a certain afternoon in Paris.

I happened to be walking along the Boulevard to my hotel. The big gun had been throwing its shells into the city all day. Suddenly one fell so close to where I was walking that it broke the windows around me, and I was nearly thrown to my feet. In my soul I cursed the Hun, as all who have lived in Paris finally come to be doing as each shell bursts. But I had more reason to curse than I knew at that moment.

The people were running into a side street, the next one toward which I was approaching. I followed the crowd. My uniform got me past the gendarmes in through a little court, up a pair of stairs where the shell had penetrated the walls of a maternity hospital.

What I saw there in that room shall make me hate the Hun forever.

New-born babes had been killed, a nurse and two mothers. When I thought of the expectant homes into which those babes had come, when I thought of the fathers at the front who would never see again either their wives or those new babies, when I saw the blood that smeared the plaster and floors of that room, when I saw the little twisted baby beds, a flush of hatred swept over me, as it did over all who saw it, a new birth of hatred that could never die until those little babies and those mothers and the nurse are avenged. That is a Silhouette of Sacrilege that makes the gamut complete.

There was the desecration of the holy sanctuaries; there was the desecration of the graves of brave soldiers of France; there was the derision of his bronze cross; there was the desecration of the most sacred day in Christendom, Good Friday, and then the desecration of little children, mothers of new-born babes, and nurses. Could the case be more complete? Could Silhouettes of Sacrilege cover a wider gamut of hatred and disgust than these silhouettes picture?

VI
SILHOUETTES OF SILENCE

Two o'clock in the morning on the sea is sometimes cold and disagreeable, and sometimes it is glorious with wonder and beauty. But whether it is beautiful or whether it is cold and disagreeable, at that exact hour in the war zone on every American transport, now, every boy is summoned on deck until daylight. This is only one of the many precautions that the navy is taking to save life in case of a U-boat attack. One thing that ought to comfort every mother and father in America is the care that is manifested and the precautions that are taken by the navy in getting the soldiers to France. One of the most thrilling chapters of the history of this war, when it is written, will be that chapter. And one of the most wonderful, the most colossal feats will be the safe transportation overseas of those millions of soldiers with so little loss of life while doing it.

And one of the best precautions is this of getting every boy up out of the hold and out of the staterooms, officers and all, on deck, standing by the assigned life-boats and rafts. Not a single boy remains below in the war zone.

Day is just breaking across the sea. It is a beautiful dawning. Five thousand American boys line the railings of a certain great transport. They are not allowed to smoke. They do not sing. They do not talk much. Some of them are sleepy, for the average American boy is not used to being awakened at two in the morning. They just stand and wait and watch through five hours of silence as the great ship plunges its way defiantly through the danger zone, saying in so many words: "We're ready for you!"

And the silhouette of that great ship, lined with khaki-clad American boys, waiting, watching, as seen from another transport, where the watcher who writes this story stands, is a sight never to be equalled in art or story. To see the huge bulk of a great transport just a stone's throw away, moving forward, without a sound from its rail-lined, soldier-packed deck, is one of the striking Silhouettes of Silence.

Thomas Carlyle once said of man: "Stands he not thereby in the centre of Immensities, in the conflux of Eternities?" One day I saw the American army standing "in the centre of immensities, in the conflux of eternities," at the focus of histories. One day I saw the American army in France march in answer to General Pershing's offer to the Allies at the beginning of the big drive, march to its place in history beside its Allies, the English and the French.

The news came. The first division of American troops was to leave overnight and march overland into the Marne line. Our Allies needed us. They had called. We were answering.

As a tribute to the efficiency of the American army, may I say that the one well-trained, seasoned division of troops that we had in a certain quiet sector picked up bag and baggage overnight and, like the Arabs, "silently stole away," and did it so well and so efficiently that not even the Y. M. C. A. secretaries, who had been living with this division intimately for months, knew that they were gone, and that a new division had taken its place, until the next morning. Talk about German efficiency—that phrase, "German efficiency," has become a bugaboo to frighten the world. American efficiency is just as great, if not greater.

I saw that division marching overland. It was a thrilling sight. Coming on it suddenly, and looking down upon its marching columns from the brow of a hill, and then riding past it in a Ford camionet all day long with Irving Cobb, riding past its ammunition-wagons, past its machine-gun battalion, past its great artillery company, past its hundreds of infantrymen, past its trucks, past its clean-cut officers astride their horses, past its supply-trains, past its flags and banners, past its kitchen-wagons, seeing it stop to eat, seeing it shoulder its rifles, seeing its ambulances and its Red Cross groups, seeing its khaki-clad American boys wind through the valleys and up the hills and over the bridges (the white stone bridge), through its villages, many in which American soldiers had never been seen before; welcomed by the people as the saviors of France, seeing its way strewn with the flowers of spring by little children, and with the welcome and the tears of French mothers and daughters clad in black, seeing it march along the French streams from early morning until late at night, this was a sight to stir the pride of any American to the point of reverence.

But all day as we rode along that winding trail I thought of the song that the soldiers are singing, "There's a Long, Long Trail Awinding to the Land of Our Dreams," and when I looked into the faces of those American boys I saw there the determination that the trail that they were taking was a trail that, although it was leading physically directly away from home, and toward Berlin, yet it was, to their way of thinking, the shortest way home. The trail that the American army took that day as it marched into the Marne line was the "home trail," and every boy marched that road with the determination that the sooner they got that hard job ahead over with, the sooner they would get home. I talked with many of them as they stopped to rest and found this sentiment on every lip.

But it was a silent army. I heard no singing all day long—not a song. Men may sing as they are marching into training-camps; they may sing when they board the boats for France now; they may sing as they march into rest-billets, but they were not singing that day as they marched into the great battle-line of Europe.

I heard no laughter. I heard no loud talking, I heard no singing; I heard only the tramp, tramp, tramp of marching feet, and the crunching of the great motor-trucks, and the patter of horses as the officers galloped along their lines. That army of American men knew that the job on which they were entering was not child's play. They knew that democracy depended upon what they did in that line. They knew that many of them would never come back. They knew that at last the real thing was facing them. They were not like dumb, driven beasts. They were men. They were American men. They were thinking men. They were silent men. They were brave men.

They were marching to their place in history unafraid, and unflinching, but thoughtful and silent.

Another Silhouette of Silence. It was after midnight on the Toul line. We were driving back from the front. The earth was covered with a blanket of snow. Everything was white. We were moving cautiously because with the snow over everything it was hard to tell where the icy road left off and the ditches began; and those ditches were four feet deep, and a big truck is hard to get out of a hole. Then there were no lights, for we were too near the Boche batteries.

"Halt!" rang out suddenly in the night, and a sentry stepped into the middle of the road.

I got down to see what he wanted.

"There are fifty truck-loads of soldiers going into the trenches to-night, and they are coming this way. Drive carefully, for it is slippery."

In a few moments we came to the first truck filled with soldiers, and passed it. A hundred yards farther we came to the second one, loaded down with American boys. Their rifles were stacked in the front of the truck, and their helmets made a solid steel covering over the trucks. One by one, fifty trucks loaded with American soldiers passed us. One can hardly imagine that many American boys anywhere without some noise, but the impressive thing about that scene was that not a single word, not a sound of a human voice, came from a single one of those fifty trucks. The only sound to be heard breaking the silence of the night was the crunching of the chained wheels of the heavy trucks in the snow. We watched that strangely silent procession go up over a snow-covered hill and disappear. Not a single sound of a human voice had broken the silence.

Another Silhouette of Silence: It is an operating-room in an evacuation hospital. The boy was brought in last night. An operation was immediately imperative. I had known the boy, and was there by courtesy of the major in charge of the hospital. The boy had asked that I come.

For just one hour they worked, two skilled American surgeons, whose names, if I were to mention them, would be recognized as two of America's greatest specialists. France has many of them who have given up their ten-thousand-dollar fees to endure danger to save our boys. During that hour's stress and strain, with sweat pouring from their brows, they worked. Now and then there was a nod to a nurse, who seemed to understand without words, and a motion of a hand, but not three words were spoken. It made a Silhouette of Silence that saved a boy's life.

The next scene is a listening-post. Two men are stretched on their stomachs in the brown grass. A little hole, just enough to conceal their bodies, has been dug there. The upturned roots of an old tree that a bursting shell had desecrated was just in front. "Tap! Tap! Tap!" came the sounds of Boches at work somewhere near and underground. It is needless to say that this was a Silhouette of Silence, and that a certain Y. M. C. A. secretary was glad when it was all over and he got back where he belonged.

[Illustration: The upturned roots of an old tree were just in front.]

The beautiful columns of the Madeleine bask under the moonlight. Paris was never so quiet. The silence of eternity seemed to have settled down over her. As one looked at the Madeleine under that magical white moonlight he imagined that he had been transported back to Athens, and that he was no longer living in modern times and in a world at war. It was all so quiet and peaceful, with a great moon floating in the skies——

But what is that awful wail that suddenly smites the stillness as with a blow? It seems like the wailing of all the lost souls of the war. It sounds like the crying of the more than five million sorrowing women there are left comfortless in Europe. It is the siren. An air-raid is on. The "alert" is sounding. The bombs begin to fall. The Boches have gotten over even before the barrage is up. Hell breaks loose for an hour. No battle on the front ever heard more terrific cannonading than the next hour. The barrage was the heaviest ever sent up over Paris. The six Gothas that got over the city dropped twenty-four bombs.

The terrific bombardment, however, now as one looks back, only serves to make the preceding silence stand out more emphatically, and the Madeleine, basking in the moonlight the hour before, more beautiful in its silhouette of grace and bulk against the golden light.

A month on the front lines with thunder beating always, a month of machine-gun racket, a month of bombing by Gothas every night, a month of crunching wheels, a month of pounding motors and rumbling trucks, a month of marching men, a month of the pounding of horses' hoofs on the hard roads of France, a month of sirens and clanging church-bells in the *tocsin*, and then a day in the valley of vision, down at Domremy where Jeanne d'Arc was born, was a contrast that gave a Silhouette of Silence to me.

One day on the Toul line, a train by night, and the next morning so far away that all you could hear was the singing of birds. Peasants quietly tended their flocks. Children played in the roads. The valley was beautiful under the sunlight of as warm and as beautiful a spring day as ever fell over the fields of France. I stood on the very spot where the peasant girl of Orleans caught her vision. I looked down over the valley with "the green stream streaking through it," with silence brooding over it, a bewildering contrast with the day and the month that had just preceded; and it all stands out as one of the Silhouettes of Silence.

Another day, another hour, another part of France. They call it "Calvaire." It covers several acres. The peasants go there to worship in pilgrimage every year. There is a Garden of Gethsemane, with marvellous statues built life-size. Then through the woods there is a worn pathway to the Sanhedrin. This is of marble. Jesus is here before his accusers in marble statuary.

As his accusers question him and he answers them not, they wonder. But those who have seen "Calvaire" in France do not wonder, for from that room there is a clean swath of trees cut, and a quarter of a mile away looms, on a hill, a real Calvary, with the tree crosses silhouetted against the sky, and Jesus is seeing down the pathway the hill of the cross.

Then there is "The Way of the Cross," built by peasant hands. It is a road covered with flintstones as sharp as knives. This flint road must be a mile long, and it winds here and there leading to Calvary, and along its way are the various stations of the cross in life-size figures. Jesus is seen at every step of this agony bearing his cross until relieved by Simon. Over this flintstone every year the people come by thousands, and crawl on their naked knees or walk on their naked feet. Every stone is stained with blood; stumbling, cruelly hurt, bleeding, they go "The Way of the Cross," and I have no doubt but that they go back to their homes better men and women for having done so.

The day that we went to "Calvaire" it was a fitful June afternoon. As we walked along "The Way of the Cross," across the field, past the living, almost breathing, statues of the Master bearing his cruel cross, past the sneering figures of those who hated him, and past the weeping figures of those who loved and would aid him, and as we came to the hill itself, suddenly black clouds gathered behind it and rain began to pour.

"I am glad the clouds are there back of Calvary. I am glad it is raining as we climb the hill of Calvary. I am willing to be soaked. It seems more fitting so, with the black clouds there and all. It reminds me of 'The Return from Calvary' in the painting," one of the party said impressively.

Up the winding hill we climbed, and there gaunt and cruel against a sombre sky stood the three crosses, just as we have always imagined them. The hill was so high that it overlooked as beautiful a valley as I had seen in all France. It was in Brittany, as yet untouched by the war as far as its fields are concerned (not so its men and its women and its homes); but on that spring day as we looked down from the hill of Calvary we could see off in the distance the tomb, with the stone rolled away, and life-size angels standing there with uplifted wings. Then farther along the road, perhaps another quarter mile away, on another hill, were the figures of the disciples, and the women watching the ascension with rapt faces, and a glory shone round about them all.

And as we stood there on that Calvary, built in memory of the crucifixion and resurrection and ascension of their Master by the peasants, and looked down over the earth, bright with crimson poppies everywhere in field and hill, brilliant with the old-gold blossom of the broom flower, as we stood there, our hearts subdued to awe and wonder, looking down, suddenly the rain ceased and the sun shone in its full glory and lighted anew the white marble of the figures of the ascension far below us in the field.

As we stood there the thought came to me:

"So is the Christian world standing today on the hill of 'Calvaire.' The storms have been black about the Christian world. The clouds have seemed impenetrable. The earth has been desolate. We have walked on our hands and knees and in our bare feet up the flinty road of Baupaume, 'the saddest road in Christendom,' and along this road we have borne the cross. We, the Christian world, the mothers, the fathers, the little children, have bled. We have stumbled and fallen along the way. And when we climbed the hill of Calvary, as we have been doing for these years of war, the clouds darkened and we saw only the ominous silhouettes of the three crosses.

"But the sun is now breaking the clouds, and it shall burn its way to a glorious day. Across the fields we see the open tomb and the resurrection is about to dawn; the day of brotherhood, democracy, justice, love, and peace forever.

"Hope is in the world, hope brooding, hope dominant, hope triumphant, hope in its supreme ascension."

One could not see this Silhouette of Silence, this "Calvaire" of the French nation, and not come away knowing the full meaning of the war. It is "The New Calvary" of the world.

VII
SILHOUETTES OF SERVICE

A newspaper paragraph in a Paris paper said: "Dale was last seen in a village just before the Germans entered it, gathering together a crowd of little French children, trying to get them to a place of safety."

Dale has never been seen since, and that was two months ago. Whether he is dead or alive we do not know, but those who knew this manly American lad best, say unanimously: "That was just like Dale; he loved kids, and he was always talking about his own and showing us their pictures."

No monument will ever be erected to Dale, for he was just a common soldier; but I for one would rather have had the monument of that simple paragraph in the press despatches; I for one would rather have it said of me, "The last seen of Dale he was gathering together a crowd of little children"; I would rather have died in such a service than to have lived to be a part of the marching army that is one day to enter the streets of Berlin. That was a man's way to die; dying while trying to save a crowd of little children from the cowardly Hun.

[Illustration: "The last seen of Dale he was gathering together a crowd of little children."]

If I had died in that kind of service, in my dying moments I could have heard the words of John Masefield from "The Everlasting Mercy" singing in my heart:

"Whoever gives a child a treat
Makes joybells ring in Heaven's street;
Whoever gives a child a home,
Builds palaces in Kingdom Come;
Whoever brings a child to birth,
Brings Saviour Christ again to earth."

Or, better, I would have seen the Master blessing little children, taking them up in His arms and saying to the Hebrew mothers that stood about with wondering eyes: "Suffer the little children to come unto me, and forbid them not, for of such is the kingdom of heaven."

And perhaps I should have heard the echo of Joaquin Miller's sweet interpretation of that scene, for when men die, strange, sweet memories, old hymns and verses, old faces, all come back:

"Then lifting His hands He said lowly,
Of such is my Kingdom, and then
Took the little brown babes in the holy
White hands of the Savior of men;
Held them close to His breast and caressed them;
Put His face down to theirs as in prayer;
Put His cheek to their cheeks; and so blessed them
With baby hands hid in His hair."

And I am certain that last of all I should have heard the voice of the Master himself saying:

"Insomuch as ye have done it unto the least of one of these little ones, my children, ye have done it unto me."

Thank God for a death like that. One could envy such a passing, a passing in the service to little children.

I have seen some of the most magnificent episodes of service on the part of men in France, scenes that have thrilled me to the bone.

I know a Protestant clergyman in France who walked five miles on a rainy February day to find a rosary for a dying Catholic boy.

I know a Y. M. C. A. secretary who in America is the general secretary of one of the largest organizations in one of the largest Eastern cities. He has always had two hobbies: one is seeing men made whole, and the other has been fighting cigarettes. Never bigger fists or more determined fists pounded down the walls that were building themselves up around

American youth in the cigarette industry. He was militant from morning till night in his crusade against cigarettes. Some of his friends thought he was a fanatic. He even lost friends because of his uncompromising antagonism to the cigarette.

But the last time I heard of him he was in a front-line dugout. This was near Château-Thierry. The boys were coming and going from that awful fight. Men would come in one day and be dead the next. He had been with them for months, and they had come to love him in spite of his fighting their favorite pastime. They knew him for his uncompromising antagonism to cigarettes. They loved him none the less for that because he did not flinch. Neither was he narrow about selling them. He sold them because it was his duty, but he hated them.

Then for three days in the midst of the Château-Thierry fighting the matches played out. Not a match was to be had for three days. The boys were frantic for their smokes, for the nervous strain was greater than anything they had suffered in their lives. The shelling was awful. The noise never ceased. Machine-gun fire and bombing by planes at night kept up every hour. They saw lifelong friends fall by their sides every hour of the day and night. They needed the solace of their smokes.

Their secretary found two matches in his bag. He lit a cigarette for a boy, and the match was gone. Then he used the other one. Then he did a magnificent piece of service for which his name shall go down forever in the memory of those lads. Forever shall he hold their affections in the hollow of his hands. He proved to those boys that his sense of service was greater than his prejudices. He kept three cigarettes going for two days and two nights on the canteen beside him, smoking them himself in order that that crowd of boys, coming and going into the battle, in and out of the underground dugout, might have a light for the cigarettes during the few moments of respite that they had from the fight.

What a thrill went down the line when that news got to the boys out there in the woods fighting. One boy told me that a fellow he told wept when he heard it. Another said: "Good old ——! I knew he had the guts!" Another said: "I'll say he's a man!" Another came in one evening and said: "I'm going to quit cigarettes from now. If you're that much of a man, you're worth listening to!" Another said: "If I get out of this it's me for the church forever if it has that kind of men in it!"

Is it any wonder that they brought their last letters to him before they went into the trenches? Is it any wonder that they asked him for a little prayer service one night before they went into the trenches? Is it any wonder that they love him and swear by him?

Is it any wonder that when one of them was asked how they liked their secretary, the boy said: "Great! He's a man!"

Is it any wonder that when another boy was asked if their secretary was very religious, responded in his own language: "Yes, he's as religious as hell, but he's a good guy anyhow!"

That kind of service will win anybody, and that is exactly the kind of service that the boys of the American army, your boys, are getting all over France from big, heroic, unprejudiced, fatherly, brotherly men, who are willing to die for their boys as well as to live for them and with them down where the shells are thickest and the dangers are constant.

More than a hundred Y. M. C. A. men gassed and wounded to date, and more than six killed. One friend of mine stepped down into his cellar one morning, got a full breath of gas, and was dead in two minutes. There had been a gas-raid the day before, and the gas had remained in the cellar. Another I know stayed in his hut and served his men even though six shell fragments came through the hut while he was doing it. Another I know lived in a dugout for three months, under shell fire every day. One day a shell took off the end of the old château in which he was serving the men. His dugout was in the cellar. But he did not leave. Another day another shell took off the other end of the château, but he did not leave. He had no other place to go, and the boys couldn't leave, so why should he go just because he could leave if he wished? That was the way he looked at it. One man whom I interviewed in Paris, a Baptist clergyman, crawled four hundred yards at the Château-Thierry battle with a young lieutenant, dragging a litter with them across a stubble wheat-field under a rain of machine-gun bullets and shells, in plain view of the Germans, and rescued a wounded colonel. When they brought him back they had to crawl the four hundred yards again, pushing the litter before them inch by inch. It took them two hours to get across that field. A piece of shrapnel went through the secretary's shoulder. He is nearly sixty years of age, but he did not stop when a service called him that meant the almost certain loss of his own life.

I know another secretary, Doctor Dan Poling, a clergyman, and Pest, a physical director, who carried a wounded German, who had two legs broken, through a barrage of German shells across a field to safety.

But all the Silhouettes of Service are not in the front lines.

There are two divisions to the army. They used to be "The Zone of Advance" and "The Zone of the Rear." Now they call the second division "The Services of Supplies." All the men who are not in the actual fighting belong to "The Services of Supplies."

"How many men does it take to keep one pilot in the machine flying out over those waters to guard the transports in?" I asked the young ensign in charge of a seaplane station.

"Twenty-eight," he replied. "There are twenty-eight men back of every machine and every pilot."

The service that these men render, although it is hard for them to see it, is just as real and just as heroic as the service of those in the front lines. The boys in "The Services of Supplies" are eager to get up front. I have had the joy of making them see in their huts and camps that their service is supremely important.

One cannot tell what service is more important.

When I landed at Newport News, the first sound that I heard was the machine-gun hammering of thousands of riveters building ships. I know how vital that service is to the boys "over there." They could not live without the ships.

Then I came from Newport News to Washington, on my way home, and we entered that great city by night. The Capitol dome was flooded with light. As I looked at it I said to myself: "To-day from this city emanates the light of the world. The eyes of the whole of humanity are turned toward this city. That lighted dome is symbol of all this."

As I looked out of the train window as we entered Washington from Richmond, Virginia, I thought: "Surely not the shipbuilding but the ideals that go out from the Capitol are the most important 'Services of Supplies.'"

The next morning I was in Pittsburgh. As my train pulled into that great city, all along the Ohio River I saw great armies of laboring men going and coming from work. As one tide of humanity flowed out of the mills across the bridges, another flowed in, and I said: "Surely not the shipbuilders, nor the ideal-makers at Washington, but this great army of laboring men in America forms the most important part of 'The Services of Supplies'!"

Then I came to New York. In turn I spoke before two significant groups of men and women. One was a group of women meeting each day to make Red Cross bandages, and knowing the scarcity of such in France, and knowing how at times nurses have had to tear up their skirts to bandage wounds of dying boys, I said: "Surely this is it!"

Then I spoke before the artists of New York, with Mr. Charles Dana Gibson heading them, and as I had seen their stirring posters everywhere arousing the nation to action, and knew what an important part the artists and writers in France had played in "The Services of Supplies," I said: "Surely these are the most important!"

But I have found at last that none of these are the most important of all. There is another section to "The Services of Supplies," and that is more important than the mechanic behind the pilot, more important than the man who assembles the motor trucks and the ambulances in France, more important than the ship-builders, more important than the lawmakers themselves, more important even than the President, more important than that great army of laborers which I saw in Pittsburgh, more important than the artists and the Red Cross workers, and that supreme and important part of the great "Services of Supplies" is the father and mother, the wife, the child, the home, the church, the great mass of the common thinking, feeling, suffering, praying, hoping people of America. If these fail, all fails. If these lose faith and courage and hope, all lose faith and courage and hope. If these grow faint-hearted, all before them lose heart. These are they who furnish the real sinews of war. These are they who must furnish the morale, the love, the letters, the prayers, the support to both government and soldier. Yes, the common folks over here at home, I have seen clearly, are the most important part of the great division of the army that we call "The Services of Supplies." May we never fail the boy in France.

These are the Silhouettes of Service.

VIII
SILHOUETTES OF SORROW

I wondered at his hold on the hearts of the boys in a certain hospital in France. It was a strange thing. I went through the hospital with him and it seemed to me, judging by the conversation with the boys in the hundreds of cots, that he had just done something for a boy, or he was just in the process of doing something, or he was just about to do something.

They called him "daddy."

All day long I wondered at his secret, for he was so unlike any man I had seen in France in the way he had won the hearts of the boys. I was curious to know. Something in his eyes made me think of Lincoln. They had a look like Lincoln in their depths.

That night when I was about to leave I blunderingly stumbled on his secret. About the only ornament in his bare pine room in the hut was a picture on the desk. I seized on it immediately, for next to a sweet-faced baby about the finest thing on earth to look at is a boy between five and twelve. And here were two, dressed in plaid suits, with white collars, tousled hair, clean, fine American boys.

I exclaimed as I picked the picture up:

"What a fine pair of lads!"

Then I knew that I had, unwittingly, stumbled into his secret, for a look of infinite pain swept over his face.

"They are both dead. Last August wife called me on the phone and said that something awful had happened to the boys. They were all we had, and I hurried home.

"They had gone out on a Boy Scout picnic. The older had gone in swimming in the river and had gotten beyond his depth. The younger went in after him and both were drowned."

"I'm sorry I brought it back," I said humbly.

He didn't notice what I said, but went on.

"Wife and I were broken-hearted. There didn't seem much to live for. We had lost all. Then came this Y. M. C. A. work, and we thought that we would like to come over here and do for all the boys in the army what we could not do for our own. And now wife and I are here, and every time I do something for a wounded boy in this hospital, I feel as if I were serving my own dear lads."

"And you are," I said. "And if the mothers and fathers of America know that men and women of your type are here looking after their lads it will give them a new sense of comfort and you will be serving them also."

"And my wife," he added. "You know the boys up at —— call her 'The Woman with the Sandwiches and Sympathy.' She got her name because one night a drunken soldier staggered into the hut and asked for her. He didn't remember her name, but she had darned his socks, she had written letters for him, she had mothered him, she had tried to help him. They wanted to put the poor lad out, but he insisted upon seeing my wife. Finally, in desperation, seeing that he couldn't think of her name, he said, 'Wan' see that woman wif sandwiches and sympathy,' and after that the name stuck."

[Illustration: "The boys call her 'The Woman with Sandwiches and Sympathy.'"]

And as we knelt in prayer together there in the hut and I arose to clasp his hand in sympathy, I knew that through service there in France, through service to your sons, mothers and fathers of America, this brave man, as well as his wife, were solacing their grief. They were conquering sorrow in service, thank God.

Yes, there are Silhouettes of Sorrow, but these silhouettes always have back of them the gold of a new dawn of hope. They are black silhouettes, but they have a glorious background of sunrise and hope. I tell of no sorrows here that are not triumphant sorrows, such as will hearten the whole world to bear its sorrow well when it comes, pray God.

Up at —— on the beautiful Loire is my friend the secretary. It is a humble position, and there are not many soldiers there, but he is serving and brothering, tenderly and faithfully, the few that are there. No one would ever think of him as a hero, but I do. He, too, is a hero who is conquering sorrow in service.

His only daughter had been accepted for Y. M. C. A. service in France. She was all he had. He was a minister at home, and had given up his church for the duration of the war. Both were looking forward with keen anticipation to her coming to France. Then came the cable of her death.

I was there, the morning it arrived, to preach for him. He said no word to me about the blow. We went on with the service as usual. I noticed that no hymns had been selected, and that things were not in very good order for the service. I was a little annoyed at this, but I am thankful with all my heart this day that I said nothing. I had decided in my heart that he was not a very efficient religious director until I heard the next day.

When I asked him why he had not told me, he said a characteristic thing: "I didn't want to spoil the service. I thought I would keep my grief in my own heart and fight it out alone."

And fight it out he did. Letters kept coming for several weeks after the cable, letters full of girlish hope about France, and full of joy at the thoughts of seeing "daddy" soon. This was the hardest of all. He could not tear up those precious letters. Her last words and thoughts were treasures; all that he had left; but they were spear-thrusts of pain also. But bravely he fought out his battle of grief, and tenderly he ministered, mothers and fathers of America, to your boys. Is it any wonder that they loved him, that they went to him with their loneliness and their heartaches; is it any wonder that he understood all the troubles that they brought and that they bring to him?

And then there was the young secretary who had just landed in France. It had been hard to leave home, especially hard to leave that little tot of a six-year-old girl, the apple of his eye.

Some of us who have such experiences will understand this story; some of us who remember what the parting from loved ones meant when we went to France. One such I remember vividly.

There was the night before in the hotel in San Francisco, when "Betty," six-year-old, said, "Don't cry, mother. Be brave like Betty," and who even admonished her daddy in the same way, "Don't cry, daddy! Be brave like Betty!" for it was just as hard for the daddy to keep the tears back, as he thought of the separation, as it was for the mother.

Then the daddy would say to the mother: "I feel ashamed of myself to cry when I think of the thousands of daddies and husbands who are leaving their homes, not for six months' or a year's service, but 'for the period of the war,' and leaving with so much more of a cloud hanging over them than I. I have every hope that I will be back with you in six or eight months, but they——"

"Yes, but your own grief will make you understand all the better what it means to the daddies in the army who leave their babies and their wives, and oh, dear, be good to them!"

Then there was the next morning at the Oakland pier as the great transcontinental train pulled out, when the little six-year-old lady for the first time suddenly saw what losing her daddy meant. She hadn't visualized it before. Consequently, she had been brave, and had even boasted of her bravery. But now she had nothing to be brave about, for as the train started to move she suddenly burst into sobs and started down the platform after the train as fast as her sturdy little legs could carry her, crying between sobs, "Come back, daddy! Come back to Betty! Don't go away!" with her mother after her.

The daddy had no easy time as he watched this tragedy of childhood from the observation-car. It was a half-hour before he dared turn around and face the rest of the sympathetic passengers.

Going back on the ferry to San Francisco the weeping did not cease. In fact it became contagious, for a kindly old gentleman, thinking that the little lady was afraid of the boat, said: "What's the matter, dear? Are you afraid?"

"No, sir, I'm not afraid; but my daddy's gone to France, and I want him back! I want my daddy! I want my daddy!" and the storm burst again. Then here and there all over the boat the women wept. Here and there a man pulled a handkerchief out of his pocket and pretended to blow his nose.

And so we understand what it meant to this young secretary when, upon landing in France, he got the cable telling of the death of his baby girl.

At first he was stunned by the blow.

Then came a brave second cable from his wife telling him that there was nothing that he could do at home; to stay at his contemplated task of being a friend to the boys.

The brave note in the second cable gave him new spirit and new courage, and in spite of a heavy heart he went into a canteen, and will any wonder who read this story that he has won the undying devotion of his entire regiment by his tireless self-sacrificing service to the American boys?

What triumphs these are, what triumphs over sorrow and pain.

All of France is filled with these Silhouettes of Sorrow, but each has a background of triumphant, dawning light.

There was the woman and child that I saw in the Madeleine in Paris, both in black. They walked slowly up the steps and in through the great doors to pray for their daddy aviator, who had been killed a year before.

A man at the door told me that every day they come, that every day they keep fresh the memory of their loved one.

"But why does she come so long after he is dead?" I asked.

"She comes to pray for the other aviators," he added simply.

It was a tremendous thing to me. I went into the great, beautiful cathedral and reverently knelt beside them in love and thankfulness that no harm had come to my own wife and baby. But the memory of that woman's brave pilgrimage of prayer each day for a year, "for the other aviators," the picture of the woman and child kneeling, etched its way into my soul to remain forever.

"As I shot down through the night, falling to what I was certain was immediate death, I had just one thought," a young aviator said, as we sat talking in a hotel in Paris.

I said: "What was it?"

"I said to myself: 'What will the poor kiddie do without his dad?'"

Then there is that Silhouette of Sorrow that my friend brought back from Germany, he who was on the Peace Ship Commission, and who saw a train-load of German boys leaving a certain German town to fill in the gaps caused by the losses at Verdun; and because this sorrow is characteristic of the mother sorrow of the whole world, and especially of the American mother, and because it has a note of wonderful triumph, I tell it.

"I thought they were the hardest women in the world," he said, "for as I watched them saying farewell to their boys there wasn't a tear. There was laughter everywhere, shouting and smiles, as if those poor boys were going off to school, or to a picnic, when we all knew that they were going to certain death.

"I felt like cursing their indifference to the common impulses of motherhood. I watched a thousand mothers and women as that train started, and I didn't see a tear. They stood waving their hands and smiling until the train was out of sight. I turned in disgust to walk away when a woman near me fainted, and I caught her as she fell. Then a low moan went up all over that station platform. It was as if those mothers moaned as one. There was no hysteria, just a low moan that swept over them. I saw dozens of them sink to the floor unconscious. They had kept their grief to themselves until their lads had gone. They had sent their boys away with a smile, and had kept their heartache buried until those lads had departed."

I think that this is characteristic of the triumphant motherhood of the whole world. It is a Silhouette of Sorrow, but it has a background of the golden glory of bravery which is the admiration of all the world. A recent despatch says that a woman, an American, sent her boy away smiling a few weeks ago, and then dropped dead on the station, dead of grief.

One who has lived and worked in France has silhouette memories of funeral processions standing out in sombre blackness against a lurid nation. He has memories of funeral trains in little villages and in great cities; he has memories of brave men standing as doorkeepers in hotels, with arms gone, with crosses for bravery on their breasts, but somehow the cloud of sorrow is always fringed with gold and silver. He has memories of funeral services in Notre Dame and the Madeleine, and in little towns all over France, but in and around them all there is somewhere the glory of sunlight, of hope, of courage. Indeed, one cannot have silhouettes, even of sorrow, if there is no background of light and hope.

For we know that even in war-time God "still makes roses," as John Oxenham, the English poet, tells us:

"Man proposes—God disposes;
Yet our hope in Him reposes
Who in war-time still makes roses."

John Oxenham, one of the outstanding poets of the war, wrote this verse, and for me it has been a sort of a motto of faith during my service in France. I have quoted it everywhere I have spoken, and it has sung its way into my heart, like a benediction with its comfort and its assurance.

It has been surprising, too, the way the boys have grasped at it. I have quoted it to them privately, in groups, and in great crowds down on the line, and back in the rest-camps, and in the ports, and everywhere I have quoted it I have had many requests to give copies of it to the boys. I quoted it once in a negro hut, hesitating before I did so lest they should not appreciate it enough to make quoting it excusable. But I took a chance.

When the service was over a long line of intelligent-looking negro boys waited for me. I thought that they just wanted to shake hands, but much to my astonishment most of them wanted to know if I would give them a copy of that verse, and so I was kept busy for half an hour writing off copies of that brief word of faith.

One never quite knows all that this verse means until he has been in France and has seen the suffering, the heartache, the loneliness, the mud, and dirt and hurt; the wounds and pain and death which are everywhere.

Then he turns from all the suffering to find a blood-red poppy blooming in the field behind him; or a million of them covering a green field like a great blanket. These poppies are exactly like our golden California poppies. Like them they grow in the fields and along the hedges; even covering the unsightly railroad-tracks, as if they would hide the ugly things of life.

I thought to myself: "They look as if they had once been our golden California poppies, but that in these years of war every last one of them had been dipped in the blood of those brave lads who have died for us, and forever after shall they be crimson in memory of these who have given so much for humanity."

One day in early June I was driving through Brittany along the coast of the Atlantic. On the road we passed many old-fashioned men, and women in their little white bonnets and their black dresses.

We stopped at a beautiful little farmhouse for lunch. It attracted us because of its serene appearance and its cleanliness. A gray-haired little old woman was in the yard when we stopped our machine.

The yard was literally sprinkled with blood-red poppies. As we walked in and were making known our desire for lunch a beautiful girl of about twenty-five, dressed in mourning, stepped to the doorway, her black eyes flashing a welcome, and cried out: "Welcome, comrade Americaine." Behind her was a little girl, her very image.

I guessed at once that in this quiet Brittany home the war had reached out its devastating hand. I had remarked earlier in the day as we drove along: "It is all so quiet and beautiful here, with the old-gold broom flowering everywhere on hedge and hill, and with the crimson poppies blowing in the wind, that it doesn't seem as if war had touched Brittany."

A friend who knew better said: "But have you not noticed that women are pulling the carts, women are tilling the fields? Look at that woman over there pulling a plough. Have you not noticed that there are no men but old men everywhere?"

He was right. I could not remember to have seen any young men, and everywhere women were working in the field, and in one place a woman was yoked up with an ox, ploughing, while a young girl drove the odd pair.

"And if that isn't enough, wait until we come to the next cathedral and I'll show you what corresponds to our 'Honor Rolls' in the churches back home. Then you'll know whether war has touched Brittany or not."

We entered with reverent hearts the next ancient cathedral of Brittany, in a little town with a population of only about two thousand, we were told, and yet out of this town close to five hundred boys had been killed in the Great War. Their names were posted, written with many a flourish by some village penman. In the list I saw the names of four brothers who had been killed, and their father. The entire family had been wiped out, all but the women.

So I was mistaken. As quiet and peaceful as Brittany was during May and June, as beautiful with broom and poppies as were its fields, it had not gone untouched by the cruel hand of war. It, too, had suffered, as has every hamlet, village, and corner of fair France; suffered grievously.

Thus I was not surprised to hear that this beautiful young woman was wearing black because her husband had been killed, and that the little girl behind her in the doorway had no longer any hope that her soldier daddy would some day come home and romp with her as of old. At the lunch we were told all about it. True, there were tears shed in the telling, and these not alone by these brave Frenchwomen and the little girl, but it was a sweet, simple story of courage. Several times during its telling the little girl ran over to kiss the tears out of her mother's eyes, and to say, with such faith that it thrilled us: "Never mind, mother, the Américains are here now; they will kill the cruel Boches."

After dinner we walked amid the red poppies in the great lawn that was the crowning feature of that white-stone home. On the walls of the ancient house grew the most wonderful roses that I have ever seen anywhere, not excepting California. Great white roses, so large and fragrant that they seemed unreal, delicately moulded red roses, which unfolded like a baby's lips, climbed those ancient stone walls. The younger woman cared for them herself, and was engaged in that task of love even before we went away.

I said to her, in what French I could command: "They are the most beautiful roses I have ever seen."

"Even in your own beautiful America?" she asked with a smile.

"Yes, more beautiful even than in my own America."

"Yes," she said, "they are most beautiful, but they are more than that; they are full of hope for me. They are my promise that I shall see him some time again. They come back each spring. He loved them and cared for them when he was alive. Even on his leave in 1915 he gloried in them. And when they come back each spring they seem to come to give me promise that I shall see him again."

Then I translated Oxenham's verses about the roses for her. The translation was poor, but she caught the idea, and her face beamed with a new light, and she said: "Ah, yes, it is as I believe, that the good God who still makes the beautiful roses, he will not take him away from me forever."

I never read Oxenham's verse now that I do not see that little cottage in Brittany that has sheltered the same family for centuries; twined about with great red and white roses; and the old mother and the young mother and the little lonely girl.

> "Yet our hope in Him reposes
> Who in war-time still makes roses."

Another time, down on the Toul front lines, I had this thought forced home by a strange scene. It was in mid-March and for three days a heavy blizzard had been blowing. I, who had lived in California for several years, wondered at this blizzard and revelled in it, although I had had to drive amid its fury, sometimes creeping along at a snail's pace, without lights, down near the front lines. It was cruelly cold and hard for those of us who were in the "truck gang."

One night during this blizzard, which blew with such fury as I have never seen before, we were lost. At one time we were headed directly for the German lines, which were close, but an American sentry stopped us before we had gone very far, demanding in stern tones: "Where are youse guys goin' that direction?"

I replied: "To Toul."

"To Toul! You're going straight toward the Boche lines. Turn around. You're the third truck that's got lost in this blizzard. Back that opposite way is your direction."

The morning after it had cleared it was worth all the discomfort to see the hills and fields of France. One group of hills which I had heard were the most heavily fortified in all France, loomed like two huge sentinels before the city. The Germans knew this also, and military experts say that that is the reason why they did not try to reach Paris by this route in the beginning of the war.

We were never permitted on these hills, but we had seen them belch fire many a time as the German airplanes came over the city.

But on this morning, after three days of snow, those great black hills were transformed, covered with a pure white blanket. The trees were robed in white. Not a spot of black appeared. Even the great guns on the top of the hill looked like white fingers pointing toward Berlin. The roads and fields and hills of France had suddenly been transformed as by a magic wand into things beautiful and white.

War is black. War is muddy. War is bloody. War is gray. War is full of hate and hurt and wounds and blood and death and heartache and heartbreak and homesickness and loneliness.

Thomas Tiplady, in "The Cross at the Front," was right when he described war as symbolized by the great black cloud of smoke that unrolled in the sky when a great Jack Johnson had exploded. Everything that war touches it makes ugly, except the soul, and it cannot blacken that.

It ruins the fields and makes them torn and cut; it tears the trees into ragged stumps. It kills the grass and tramples it underfoot. It takes the most beautiful architecture in the world and makes a pile of dust and dirt of it. It takes a beautiful face and makes it horrible with the scars of bayonet and burning gases.

But on this morning God seemed to be covering up all of that ugliness and dirt and mud and blackness. Fields that the day before had been nothing but ugly blotches were white and beautiful. Ammunition dumps, horrible in their suggestion of death, seemed now to have been covered over and hidden by some kindly hand of love. The great brown-bronzed hills, the fortifications filled with death and horror were gleaming white in the morning sunlight.

I said to the other driver: "Well, it's too beautiful to be true, isn't it? It's a shame to think that when we get back from the front it will all be gone, melted, and the old mud and dirt will be back again."

"Yes, but it means something to me," he said.

"What does it mean?"

"It means the future."

"What are you talking about, man?"

"Why, it means that some day this land will be beautiful again. It means that, impossible as that idea seems, the war will cease, that people will till these fields again, that grass will grow, that flowers will bloom in these fields again, that people will come back to their homes in peace. It is symbolical of that great white peace that will come forever, when the ugly thing we call war will be buried so deeply underneath the white blanket of peace and brotherhood that the world will know war no more. It's like a rainbow to me. It is a promise."

I had never heard Tom grow so eloquent before, and what he said sounded Christian. It sounded like man's talk to me. It was the dream of the Christ I knew. It was the dream of the prophets of old. It was Tennyson's dream. Such a dream will not die from the earth, and men will just keep on dreaming it until some day it will come true, for—

"Man proposes—God disposes;
Yet my hope in Him reposes,
Who in war-time still makes roses."

The white and crimson roses of that little cottage in Brittany, the quiet and peace and promise and vision of a Jeanne d'Arc in the village of Domremy; the blooming of a billion red poppies in the fields of France; the blanketing of the earth with a covering of white snow sufficient to hide the ugliness of war, even for a day, all give promise of the God who, in the end, when he has given man every chance to redeem himself, and who, even amid cruel wars "still makes roses," will finally bring to pass "peace on earth; good-will to men."

"*Somewhere in France.*"

IX
SILHOUETTES OF SUFFERING

All night long a group of Red Cross and Y. M. C. A. men and women had been feeding the refugees from Amiens. There were two thousand of them in one basement room of the Gare du Nord. They had not eaten for forty-eight hours. Most of them were little children, old men, and women of all ages.

Two hundred or more of them had been in the hands of the Germans for two years, and when a few days before it came time for the Germans to open their second big Somme drive, they had driven these women and little girls out ahead of them, saying: "Go back to the French now, we do not want you any longer."

For two days and nights these refugees had tramped the roads of France without food, many of them carrying little babies in their arms, all of them weary and sick near unto death.

The little children gripped your heart. As you handed them food and saw their little claw-like hands clutch at it, and as you saw them devour it like starved animals, the while clutching at a dirty but much-loved doll, somehow you could not see for the mists in your eyes as you walked up and down the narrow aisles of that crowded basement pouring out chocolate and handing out food. The things you saw every minute in that room hung a veil over your eyes, and you were afraid all the while that in your blinding of tears you would step on some sleeping, starving child, who was lying on the cold floor in utter exhaustion, regardless of food.

One woman especially attracted me. I noticed her time and time again as I walked past her with food. She was lying on her back on the floor, with nothing under her, her arms thrown back over her head, a child in her arms, or rather, lying against her breast asleep. She looked like an educated, cultured woman. Her features were beautiful, but she looked as if she had passed through death and hell in suffering. I asked her several times as I passed by if she wouldn't have some food, and each time she gave some to her baby but took none herself. She could hardly lift her body from the stone basement to feed the child, and feeling that the thing that she needed most herself was food, I urged her to eat, but she would not.

Finally I stopped before her and asked her if she was ill. She looked up into my face and said: "Très fatiguée, monsieur! Très fatiguée, monsieur!" (Very weary, sir! Very weary, sir!)

By morning she was rested and accepted food. Then she told me her story. Two days before in her village they had been ordered by the army to leave their homes in a half-hour; everybody must be gone by that time; the Germans were coming, and there was no time to lose. She had hastily gathered some clothes together. The baby was lying in its crib. Her other child, a little six-year-old girl, had gone out into the front of the home watching for the truck that was to gather up the village people. A bomb fell from a German Gotha and killed this child outright, horribly mangling her body. This suffering mother just had time to pick the little mangled body up and lay it on a bed, kiss its cheeks good-by and leave it there, for there was no other way. She did not even have the satisfaction of burying her child.

"Very weary! Very weary!" I can hear her words yet: "Très fatiguée! Très fatiguée!" No wonder you were fatigued, mother heart. You had a right to be, weary unto death. No wonder you did not care to eat all that long horrible night in the Gare du Nord.

Loneliness is naturally one of the things with which our own boys suffer most. When one remembers that these Americans of ours are thousands of miles away from their homes, most of them boys who have never been away from home in their lives before; most of them boys who have never crossed the ocean before, they will judge fairly and understand better the loneliness of the American soldier. It is not a loneliness that will make him any the less a soldier. Ay, it is because of that very home love, and that very eagerness to get back to his home, that he will and does fight like a veteran to get it over.

"Gosh! I wish I would find just one guy from Redding!" a seventeen-year-old boy said to me one night as I stood in a Y. M. C. A. hut. He was about the loneliest boy I saw in France. I saw that he needed to smile. He was nothing but a kid, after all.

"Gosh! I wish I'd see just one guy from San Jose!" I said with a smile. Then we both laughed and sat down to some chocolate, and had a good talk, the very thing that the lad was hungry for.

He had been in France for nearly a year and he hadn't seen a single person he knew. He had been sick a good deal of the time and had just come from an appendix operation. He was depressed in spirits, and his homesickness had poured itself out in that one phrase: "Gosh! I wish I'd see just one guy from Redding!"

Those who do not think that homesickness comes under the heading of "Suffering" had better look into the face of a truly homesick American boy in France before he judges.

The English Tommy is only a few hours from home, and knows it. The French soldier is fighting on his own native soil, but the American is fighting three thousand miles away from home, and some of them seven thousand.

"I haven't had a letter in five months from home," a boy in a hospital said to me. He was lonely and discouraged. And right here may I say to the American people that there is no one thing that needs more constant urging than the plea that you write, write, write to your soldier in France. He would rather have letters than candy, or cigarettes, or presents of any kind, as much as he loves some of these material things. I have put it to a vote dozens of times, and the result is always the same; ten to one they would rather have a letter from home than a package of cigarettes or a box of candy. I have seen boys literally suffering pangs that were a thousand times worse than wounds because they did not receive letters from those at home.

"Hell! Nobody back there cares a damn about me! I haven't received a letter in five months!" a boy burst out in my presence in Nancy one night.

"Have you no mother or sister?"

"Yes, but they're careless; they always were about letter-writing."

I tried to fix up excuses for them, but it tested both my imagination and my enthusiasm to do it. I could put no real heart into making excuses for them, and so my words fell like lame birds to the ground, and the tragedy of it was that both of us knew there was no good excuse. It was the most pitiable case I saw in France. God pity the careless mother or sister or father or friend who isn't willing to take the time and make the sacrifice that is needed to at least supply a letter three times a week to the lad who is willing to sacrifice his all, if need be, that those at home may live in peace, free from the horror of the Hun.

"Less Sweaters
And More Letters"

might very well be the motto of the folks here at home, for the boys would profit more in the long run, both in their bodies and in their souls. A censor friend of mine said to me one day: "If you ever get a chance when you go home to urge the people of America to write, and write, and write to their boys, do it with all your heart. You could do no better service to the boys than that."

"What makes you feel so keenly about it?" I asked him, for he talked so earnestly that it surprised me. Ordinarily you think of the censor as utterly devoid of humanitarian impulses, just a sort of a machine to slice out the really interesting things in your letters, a great human blue pencil, or a great human pair of scissors. But here was a censor that felt deeply what he was saying.

"I'll tell you," he replied, "it is because some of the letters that I read which are going back home from lonely boys, begging somebody to write to them; literally begging somebody, anybody, to write! It gets my goat! I can't stand it. I often feel like adding a sentence to some letters myself going home, telling them they ought to be ashamed the way they treat their boys about letter-writing; but the rules are so stringent that I must neither add to nor take from a letter save in the line of my duties. I'd like to tell a few of the people back home what I think of them, and I'd like for them to read some of the heartaches that I read in the letters of the boys. Then they'd understand how I feel about it."

I shall never forget my friend the wrestler when I asked how it was that he kept so clean, and he replied: "The letters help a lot."

I have seen boys suffering from wounds of every description. I have seen them lying in hospitals with broken backs. I have seen them with blinded eyes. I have seen them with legs gone, and arms. I have seen them when the doctors were dressing their wounds. I remember one captain who had fifty wounds in his back, and he had them dressed without a single cry. I have seen them gassed, and I have seen them shot to pieces with shell shock, and yet the worst suffering I have seen in France has been on the part of boys whose folks back home have neglected them; boys who, day after day, had seen the other fellows get their letters regularly, boys who had gone with hope in their hearts time after time for letters, and then had lost hope. This is real suffering, suffering that does more to knock the morale out of a lad than anything that I know in France.

Silhouettes of Suffering stand out in my memory with great vividness. One general cause of suffering in addition to the above is loneliness in the heart of the young husband and father, who has a wife and kiddie back home.

I remember one young officer that I saw in a Paris hotel. He had been out in the Vosges Mountains with a company of wood-choppers for six months. He had come in for his first leave. His leave lasted eight days. Instead of going to the theatres he sat around in our officers' hotel lobby and watched the women walking about, the Y. M. C. A. girls who were the hostesses there. They noticed him as he sat there all evening, hardly moving. After several nights one of the men secretaries went up to him and said: "Why don't you go over and talk with them? They would be glad to talk with you."

"Oh," he said, "I never was much for women at home, except my wife and kid. I never did know how to talk to women. Especially now, for I've been up in the woods for six months. Just let me sit here and look at 'em. That's enough for me. Just let me sit here and look at 'em!"

And that was the way he spent his leave, just loafing around in that hotel lobby watching the women at their work.

"This has been the loneliest day of my life," a major said to me on Mother Day in a great port of entry.

"Why, major?"

Then he reached into his pocket and pulled out the picture of a seven-year-old boy and that boy's mother.

Suffering? Yes, of course I have seen boys wounded, as I have said, but for real downright suffering, loneliness is worst, and it lies entirely within the province of the folks at home to alleviate this suffering. I have seen a boy morose and surly, discouraged and grouchy in the morning. He didn't know what was the matter with himself. In the afternoon I have seen him laughing and yelling like a wild animal at play, happy as a lark.

What was the difference? He had gotten a letter.

[Illustration: What was the difference? He had gotten a letter.]

Then there is the Silhouette of Physical Suffering. Hundreds of these sombre silhouettes stand out against a lurid background of fire and blood. One only I quote because it has a fringe of hope.

The boy's back was broken. It had been broken by a shell concussion. There were no visible signs of a wound on his body anywhere, the doctors told me in the hospital. He did not know it as yet. He thought it was his leg that was hurt. They asked me to tell him, as gently as I could. It was a hard task to give a man.

He was lying on a raised bed so that, when I went up to it, it came up to my neck almost, and when I talked with the lad I could look straight into his eyes. Those eyes I shall never forget, they were so fearless, so brave, and yet so full of weariness and suffering.

I took his hand and said: "Boy, I am a preacher." For once I didn't say anything about being a secretary. I just told him I was a preacher.

He said: "I am so glad you have come. I just wanted to see a real, honest-to-goodness preacher." He forced a smile to accompany this sentence.

"Well, I'm all of that, and proud of it," I replied, smiling back into his brave eyes.

"I'm so tired. I try to be brave, but I've been lying here for three months now, and my leg doesn't seem to get any better. It pains all the time until I think I'll die with the agony of it. I never sleep only when they give me something. But I try hard to be brave."

"You are brave!" I said to him. "They all tell me that, the doctors and nurses."

"They are so good to me." he said in low tones so that I had to bend to hear them. "But my leg; they don't seem to be able to help me."

Then I told him as gently as I could that it was not his leg, that it was his back, and that he would likely not get well. Then I tried to tell him of the room in his Father's house that was ready for him when he was ready to accept it, and of what a glorious welcome there was there.

He reached out for my hand in the semi-darkness of that evening. I can feel his hand-clasp yet. I didn't know what to say, but a phrase that had lingered in my mind from an old story came to the rescue.

"Don't you want the Christ to help you bear your pain?" I asked him.

"That is just what I do want," he said simply. "That was why I was so glad you came—an honest-to-goodness preacher," and he smiled again, so bravely, in spite of his suffering, and in spite of the news that I had just broken to him.

Then we prayed. I stood beside his bed holding his hand and praying. The room was full of other wounded boys, but in the twilight I doubt if a lad there knew what we were doing. I spoke low, just so he could hear, and the Master knew what was in my heart without hearing.

When I was through I felt a pressure of his hand, and he said: "Now I feel stronger. He is helping me bear my burden. Thank you for coming, and"—then he paused for words "and—thank you for bringing Him."

Yes, there is suffering in France, suffering among our soldiers, too, but suffering that is glorified by courage.

X
SOLDIER SILHOUETTES

One night down near the front lines as we drove the great truck slowly over the icy roads, on the top of a little knoll stood a lone sentinel against a background of snow, and that is a silhouette that I shall never forget.

Another night there was a beautiful afterglow, and being a lover of the beautiful as well as a driver of a truck, I was lost in the wonder of the crimson flush against the western hills.

"Makes me homesick," said the big man beside me, whose home is in the West. "Looks for all the world like one of our Arizona afterglows."

"It is beautiful," I replied, and then we were both lost in silent appreciation of the scene before us, when suddenly we were startled witless.

"Halt!" rang out through the semi-darkness. "Who goes there?"

"Y. M. C. A." we shot back as quick as lightning, for we had learned that it doesn't pay to waste time in answering a sentinel's challenge down within sound of the German guns.

"Pass on, friends," was the grinning reply. That rascal of a sentry had caught us unawares, lost in the afterglow, and he was tickled over having startled us into astonishment.

But even though he did give us a scare, I am sure that the picture of him standing there in the middle of that French road, with his gun raised against the afterglow, will be one of the outstanding silhouettes of the memories of France.

Then there was the old Scotch dominie down at Château-Thierry, with the marines. The boys called him "Doc," and loved him, for he had been with them for eight months.

One night, in the midst of the hottest fighting in June, the old secretary thought he would go out in the night and see how the boys were getting along. He walked cautiously along the edge of the woods when suddenly the word "Halt!" shot out in low but distinct tones.

"Who goes there?"

"A friend," the secretary replied.

"Oh, it's you, is it, Doc? Gee, I'm glad to see you! This is a darned weird place to-night. Every time the wind blows I think it's a Boche."

There was a slight noise out in No Man's Land. "What's that, Doc, a Boche?"

"I think not."

"You can't tell, Doc; they're everywhere. If I've seen one, I've seen ten thousand to-night on this watch."

That old gray-haired secretary will never forget that night when he walked among the men in the trenches with his little gifts and his word of cheer, that memorable night before the Americans made themselves heroes forever in the Bois du Belleau. He will never forget the sound of that boy sentry's voice when he said, "Gee, Doc, I'm glad it's you"; nor will he forget the looks of the boy as he stood there in the darkness, the guardian of America's hopes and homes, nor will he forget the firm, warm clasp of the lad's hands as he walked away to greet others of his comrades.

These are Soldier Silhouettes that remain vivid until time dies, until the "springs of the seas run dust," as Markham says:

"Forget it not 'til the crowns are crumbled;
'Til the swords of the Kings are rent with rust;
Forget it not 'til the hills lie humbled;
And the springs of the seas run dust."

No, we do not forget scenes and moments like these in our lives.

Then there is the silhouette of the profile of the captain of a certain American machine-gun company who, in March, marched with his men into the Somme line. He was an old football-player back in the States, and we were having a last dinner together in Paris, a group of college men. After dinner, when we had finished discussing the dangers of the coming weeks, and he had told us that his major had said to him, "If fifteen per cent of us come out alive, I shall be glad," and after we had drifted back to the old college days, and home and babies, and after he had shown us a picture of his wife and his kiddies, it became strangely quiet in the room, and suddenly he turned his face from us, with just the profile showing against the light of the window, and exclaimed: "My God, fellows, for a half-hour you have made me forget that there is a war, and I have been back on the old campus again playing football, and back with my babies."

Then his jaw set, and I shall never forget the profile of his face as that set look came back and once again he became the captain of a machine-gun company.

Then there was the lone church service that my friend Clarke held one evening at a crossroads of France. He had held seven services that Sunday, one in a machine-gun company's dugout, with six men; another with a group of a dozen men in a front-line trench; another with several officers in an officers' dugout; another with a battery outfit who were "On Call," expecting orders to send over a few shells; another with several men out in No Man's Land, on the sunny side of an old upturned mass of tree roots; one in a listening-post, and finally this service with a lone sentry at a crossroads.

"But how did you do it?" I asked.

"I just saw him there," Clarke replied, "and he looked lonely, and I walked up and said: 'How'd you like to have me read a little out of the Book?'

"'Fine!' he said.

"Then I prayed with him, standing there at the crossroads, and I asked him if he didn't want to pray. He was a church boy back home, and he prayed as fine a prayer as ever I heard. Then we sang a hymn together. It was 'Jesus, Lover of My Soul,' and neither of us can sing much, but as I look back on it, it was the sweetest music that I ever had a part in making. The only thing I didn't do was take up a collection. Outside of that, it was just as if we had gone through a regular church service at home. I even preached a little to him. No, not just preached, but talked to him about the Master."

"Did you even go so far with your lone one-man congregation as to have a benediction?" I asked him.

"No, I just said what was in my heart when we were through, 'God bless and keep you, boy,' and went on."

"I never heard a finer benediction than that, old man," I replied with feeling.

And the silhouette of that one Y. M. C. A. secretary holding a religious service with a lone sentry of a Sunday evening, bringing back to the lad's memory sacred things of home and church and the Christ, giving him a new hold on the bigger, better things, bringing the Christ out to him there on that road, that silhouette is mine to keep forever close to my heart. I shall see that and shall smile in my soul over it when eternity calls, and shall thank God for its sweetening influence in my life.

And so this comfort may come to the mothers and fathers of America, that through the various agencies of the American army, through General Pershing's intense interest in righteous things, through that Lincoln-like Christian leader of the chaplains, Bishop Brent, through the Y. M. C. A., and the Salvation Army, and the Knights of Columbus, your boy has his chance, whatever creed, or race, or church, to worship his God as he wishes; and not one misses this opportunity, even the lonely sentinel on the road. And the glorious thing about it is that boys who never before thought of going to church at home, crowd the huts on Sundays and for the good-night prayers on week-days.

Just before the battle of Château-Thierry, "Doc," of whom I have spoken in this chapter before, said: "Boys, do you want a communion service?"

"Yes," they shouted.

Knowing that there were Catholics and Jews and Protestants and non-believers there, he said: "Now, anybody who doesn't want to take communion may leave."

Not a single man left. Out of one hundred or more men only two did not kneel to take of the sacred bread and wine. Two Jews knelt with the others, several Roman Catholics, and men of all Protestant denominations. Half of them were dead before another sunrise came around, but they had had their service.

Every man has his opportunity to worship God in his own way and as nearly as possible at his own altars in France. There was the story of "The Rosary."

It was Hospital Hut Number ——, and half a thousand boys from the front, wounded in every conceivable way, were sitting there in the hut in a Sunday-evening service. Many of them had crutches beside them; others canes. Some of them, had their heads bandaged; others of them carried their arms in slings. Some of them had lost legs, and some of them had no arms left. Their eager faces were lighted with a strange light, such as is not seen on land or sea, and on most of those faces, unashamed, ran over pale cheeks the tears of homesickness as the young corporal whom I had taken with me from another town sang "The Rosary." I have never heard it sung with more tenderness, nor have I heard it sung in more beautiful voice. That young lad was singing his heart out to those other boys. He had not been up front himself as yet, for he was in a base port attending to his duties, which were just as important as those up front, but it was hard for him to see it that way. So he loved and respected these other lads who had, to his way of thinking, been more fortunate than he, because they had seen actual fighting. He respected them because of their wounds, and he wanted to help them. So he lifted that rich, sweet, sympathetic tenor voice until the great hut rang with the old, old song, and hearts were melted everywhere. I saw, back in the audience, a group of nurses with bowed heads. They knew what the rosary meant to those who suffer and die in the Catholic faith. They, too, had memories of that beautiful song. A group of officers, including a major, all wounded, listened with heads bowed.

As I sat on the crude stage and saw the effects of his magical voice on this crowd I got to thinking of what this war is meaning to that fine understanding of those who count the beads of the rosary and those who do not. I had seen so many examples of fine fraternal fellowship between Catholic and Protestant that I felt that I ought to put it down in some permanent form.

There is a true story of one of our Y. M. C. A. secretaries who was called to the bedside of a dying Catholic boy. There was no priest available, and the boy wanted a rosary so badly. In his half-delirium he begged for a rosary. This young Protestant Y. M. C. A. secretary started out for a French village, five miles away, on foot, to try to find a rosary for this sick Catholic boy, and after several hours' search he found a peasant woman whom he made understand the emergency of the situation, and he got the loan of the rosary and took it back through five miles of mud to the bedside of that Catholic lad, and comforted him with the feel of it in his fevered hands and the hope of it in his fevered soul. When I heard this story it stirred me to the very fountain depths, but I have seen so much of this fine spirit of service in the Y. M. C. A. since then that I have come to know that as far as the Y. M. C. A. is concerned all barriers of church narrowness are entirely swept away.

I have had most delightful comradeship since I have been in France in one great area as religious director with two Knights of Columbus secretaries and one father—Chaplain Davis—all of whom say freely and eagerly: "We have never had anything but the finest spirit of co-operation and friendship from the Y. M. C. A."

"Why," added Chaplain Davis, a Catholic priest, "why, the first Sunday I was here, when I had no place to take my boys for mass, a secretary came to me and offered me the hut. It has always been that way."

The story of the French priest who confessed a dying Catholic boy through a Y. M. C. A. Protestant secretary interpreter, in a Y. M. C. A. hut, has been told far and wide, but it is only illustrative of the broadening lines of Catholicism and the wider fraternal relations of all professed Christians.

The marvellous story that my friend, the French chaplain, tells of being marooned in a shell-hole at Verdun for several days with a Catholic priest, and of their discussion of religion and life there under shell-fire, and the tenderness with which the Catholic priest kissed the hand of the Protestant French chaplain when the two had agreed that, after all, there was one common God for a common, suffering nation of people, and that this war would break all church barriers down, and that out of it would come a new spirit in the Catholic church, a new brotherhood for all. That was an impressive indication of the thing that is sweeping France to-day in church circles, and that will sweep America after the war.

Then there is that other story of the Catholic priest who had been in the same regiment with a French Protestant chaplain, each of whom deeply respected the other because of the unflinching bravery that each had displayed under intense shell-fire, and of the great love that each had seen the other show in two years of constant warfare in the same regiment. Then came that terrible morning at Verdun, when the French Protestant chaplain, the friend of the Catholic priest, had been killed while trying to bring in a wounded Catholic boy from No Man's Land. On the day of this Protestant chaplain's funeral the Catholic priest stood in God's Acre with bared head, and spoke as tender and as sincere a eulogy as ever a man spoke over the grave of a dear friend, spoke with the tears in his eyes most of the time. Church lines were forgotten here. It was a prophetic scene, this, where a Catholic priest spoke at the funeral of a Protestant chaplain. It was prophetic of that new church brotherhood that is to come after the war is over.

XI
SKY SILHOUETTES

They are the lights, the lights of war. Sometimes they are just the stars shining out that makes the wounded soldier out in No Man's Land look up, in spite of shell-fire and thunder, in spite of wounds and death, in spite of loneliness and heartache, in spite of mud and rain, to exclaim, as Donald Hankey tells us in a most wonderful chapter of "A Student in Arms": "God! God everywhere, and underneath are the everlasting arms!"

Sometimes the Sky Silhouettes number among their own just a moonlight night with a crescent moon sailing quietly and serenely over the horizon in the east, while great guns belch fire in the west, a fire that seems to shame the timid moon itself.

Sometimes they are search-lights cleaving the sky over a great city like Paris, or along the front lines, or gleaming from an air-ship.

Sometimes they are signal-lights flashing out of the darkness from a patrolling plane overhead, or a blazing trail of fire as a patrol falls to its death in a battle by night.

Sometimes they are signal-lights flashing from an observation balloon anchored in the darkness over the trenches to guard the troops from dangers in the air.

Sometimes they are the flashes, the fleet, swallow-like flashes, of an enemy plane caught in the burning, blazing path of a search-light, and then hounded by it to its death.

Sometimes they are signals flashed from the top of a cruiser on the high seas across the storm-tossed waters to a little destroyer, which flashes back its answer, and then in turn flashes a message of light to one of the convoying planes overhead in the dim dusk of early evening.

Sometimes these Sky Silhouettes are the range-finders that poise in the air for a few seconds, guiding the air patrols home, and sometimes they are just the varied, interesting, gleaming, flashing "Lights of War."

XII
THE LIGHTS OF WAR

One's introduction into the war zone and into war-zone cities and villages, and one's visits "down the line" to the front by night, will always be filled with the thrill of the unusual because of the Lights of War. Where lights used to be, there are no lights now, and where they were not seen before the war, they are radiant and rampant now.

The first place that an American traveller notices this absence of lights is on the boat crossing over the Atlantic. From the first night out of New York the boats travel without a single light showing. Every light inside of the boat is covered with a heavy black crape, and the port-holes and windows are so scrupulously and carefully chained down that the average open-air fiend from California or elsewhere feels that he will suffocate before morning comes, and even in the bitterest of winter weather I have known some fresh-air fiends to prefer the deck of the ship, with all of its bitter winds and cold, to the inside of a cabin with no windows open. I stood on the deck of an ocean liner "Somewhere on the Atlantic" a few months ago as the great ship was ploughing its zigzag course through the black waters, dodging submarines. There was not a star in the sky. There was not a light on the boat. Absolutely the only lights that one saw was when he leaned over the railing and saw the splash of innumerable phosphorescent organisms breaking against the boat. I have seen the like of it only once before, and this was on the Pacific down at Asilomar one evening, when the waves were running fire with phosphorescence. It was a beautiful sight there and on the Atlantic too.

IT WAS MIDNIGHT

On this particular night, as far as one could see, this brilliant organic light illuminated the sea like the hands of my luminous wrist-watch were made brilliant by phosphorescence. I noticed this and looked down at my watch to see what time it was. It was midnight.

As I looked, my friend, who was standing beside me on the deck, said: "The last order is that no wrist-watches that are luminous may be exposed on the decks at night. That order came along with the order forbidding smoking on the decks at night. The Germans can sight the light of a cigar a long distance through their periscopes."

I smiled to myself, for it was my first introduction to the romantic part that lights and the lack o' lights is playing in this great World War. Then my friend continued his observations as we stood there on the aft deck watching the white waves break, glorious with phosphorescence. He said: "What a topsyturvy world it is. Three years ago if a great ship like this had dared to cross the Atlantic without a single light showing, it would have horrified the entire world, and that ship captain would have been called to trial by every country that sails the seas. He would have been adjudged insane. But now every ship sails the seas with no navigation-lights showing."

IN WAR COUNTRY

But when one gets his real introduction into the lights o' war is when he gets into the war country. It is eight o'clock in a great French city. This French city has been known the world over for its brilliant lights. It has been known for its gayly lighted boulevards, and indeed this might apply to one of three or four French cities. Light was the one scintillating characteristic of this great city. The first night that one finds himself here he feels as though he were wandering about in a country village at home. No arc-lights shine. The window-lights are all extinguished. The few lights on the great boulevards are so dimmed that their luminosity is about that of a healthy firefly in June back home. One gropes his way about, feeling ahead of him and navigating cautiously, even the main boulevards.

The first time I walked down the streets of this great city at night I had the same feeling that I had on the Atlantic. I was sailing without lights, on an unknown course, and I felt every minute that I would bump into some unseen human craft, as indeed I did, both a feminine craft and a male craft. I also had the feeling that in this particular city, in the darkness I might be submarined by a city human U-boat, which would slip up behind me. After having my second trip here I still have that feeling as I walk the streets; the unlighted streets of this city, and especially the side-streets, by night.

FRENCH CITY DURING RAID

But the one time when you catch the very heart and soul of the lights o' war is when you happen to drop into a French city while the Boches are making a raid overhead. I have had this experience in towns and villages and cities. At the signal of the siren the lights of the entire city suddenly snuff out, and the city or town or village is in total darkness. Candles may be lighted and are lighted, but on the whole one either walks the dark streets flashing his electric "Ever Ready," or huddled up in a subway or in a cellar, or in a hallway listening to the barrage of defense guns and to the bombs dropping, watches and listens and waits in total darkness, and while he waits he isn't certain half the time whether the noise he hears is the dropping of German bombs or the beating of his own heart. Both make entirely too much noise for peace and comfort.

As one approaches the front-line cities and towns he learns something more about the lights o' war. It is dark. He is in a little town and must go to another town nearer the front lines. He is standing at the depot (gare). No lights are visible save here and there an absolutely necessary red or green light, which is veiled dimly. His train pulls silently in. There is not a single light on it from one end to the other. It creeps in like a great snake. There is nobody to tell you whether this is your train or not, but you take a chance and climb into a compartment which is pitch-dark.

HEARS AMERICAN VOICE

You have a ticket that calls for first-class military compartment, but you climbed into the first open door you saw, and didn't know and didn't care whether it was first, second, third, or tenth class just so you got on your way. Your eyes soon became accustomed to the darkness and you discerned two or three forms in the seat opposite you. You wondered if they were French, Italians, Belgians, English, Australians, Canadians, Moroccans, Algerians, or Americans. It was too dark to see, but suddenly you heard a familiar voice saying, "Gosh, I wish I was back in little ole New York," and you made a grab in the darkness for that lad's hand.

All during your trip no trainman appears. You are left to your own sweet will at nights in the war zone when you are on a train. No stations are announced. You are supposed to have sense enough to know where you are going, and to have gumption enough to get off without either being assisted or told to do so. The assumption, I suppose, is that anybody who travels in the war zone knows where he is going. Personally, I felt like the American phrase, "I don't know where I'm going but I'm on the way," and I tried to jump off at two or three towns before I got to my own destination, but the American soldiers had been that way before on their way to the trenches, and wouldn't let me off at the wrong place. I thought surely that somebody would come along to take my ticket, but nobody appeared. I soon found that night trains "on the line" pay little attention to such minor matters as tickets, and I have a pocketful that have never been taken up. Time after time I have piled into a train at night, after buying a ticket to my destination; have journeyed to my destination, have gone through the depot and to my hotel without ever seeing a trainman to take the ticket. I was let severely alone. And even if a conductor had come along through the train it would have been too dark for him to have seen me, and I am sure I could have dodged him had I so desired. Maybe that's the reason they don't take the tickets up. Anyhow, I have given you a picture of a great train in the war zone, winding its way toward the front, in complete darkness.

FLASH-LIGHTS

Flash-lights have come into their own in this war. One would as soon think of living without a flash-light as he would think of travelling without clothes in Greenland. It simply cannot be done. In any city, from Paris to the smallest towns on the front, one must have his flash-light. The streets of the cities and towns of France are a hundred times more crooked than those of Boston. If Boston's streets followed the cow-paths, the streets of the cities of France followed cows with the St. Vitus dance. Around these streets one had to find his way by night with a flash-light, especially during an air-raid. One must have a flash, too, for the houses and hotels when an air-raid is on, and one must have it when one is driving a big truck or an automobile down along the front lines, for no lights are permitted on any machines, official or otherwise, after a certain point is reached. One of the favorite outdoor sports of this preacher for a month was to lie on his stomach on the front mud-guard of a big Pierce-Arrow through the war-zone roads, bumping over shell-holes, with a little pocket flash-light playing on the ground, searching out the shell-holes, and trying to help the driver keep in the road. It is a delightful occupation about two o'clock in the morning, with a blizzard blowing, and knowing that the big truck is rumbling along within sight and sound of the German big guns. Trucks make more noise on such occasions than a Twentieth Century Limited. "No lights beyond divisional headquarters" was the order, and night after night we travelled along these roads with only an occasional flash of the Ever Ready to guide. And so it is that the flash-light has come to its own, and every private soldier, officer, and citizen in France is equipped with one. He would be like a swordfish without its sword if he didn't have it.

LADDER OF LIGHT

Then suddenly you see a strange finger of light reaching into the sky. Or you may liken it to a ladder of light climbing the sky. Or you may liken it to a lance of light piercing the darkness. Or you may just call it a good, old-fashioned search-light, which it is. It is watching for Hun planes, and it plays all night long from north to south, from east to west, restlessly, eagerly, quickly, like a "hound of the heavens" guarding the earth. First it sweeps the horizon, and then it suddenly shoots straight up into the zenith like another sun, and it seems to flood the very skies. No German plane can cut through that path of light without being seen, and one night I had the rare privilege of seeing a plane caught by the search-light on its ever-vigilant patrol. It was a thrilling sight. One minute later the anti-aircraft guns were thundering away and the shrapnel was breaking in tiny patches around this plane while the search-lights played on both the plane and the shrapnel patches of smoke against the sky, making a wonderful picture. Military writers say that the enemy planes are more afraid of these search-lights than of the guns.

[Illustration: One night I had the privilege of seeing a plane caught by the search-light.]

But perhaps the most thrilling sight of all is that dark night when one sees for the first time the star-shells along the horizon. At first you may see them ten miles away making luminous the earth. Then as you drive nearer and nearer, that far-off heat-lightning effect disappears and you can actually see the curve of the star-shells as they mount toward the skies over No Man's Land and fall again as gracefully as a fountain of water. Sometimes you will see them for miles along the front, making night day and lighting up the fields and surrounding hills as though for a great celebration.

BURSTING BOMBS

The light of bursting shells as they fall, or of bursting bombs from an aeroplane, is a short, sharp, quick light like an electric flash when a wire falls or a flash of sharp lightning, but the light of the great guns along the line as they thunder their missiles of death can be seen for miles when a bombardment is on. One forgets the thunder of these belching monsters, and one forgets the death they carry, in the glory of the flame of noonday light that they make in the night.

Then there are the range-finders. These suddenly shoot up in the night, steady and clear, and remain for several minutes burning brightly before they go out. I used to see these frequently driving home from the front. They were sent up from the hangars to guide the French and American planes to a safe landing by night.

Then there is the moonlight. Moonlight nights in towns along the war front are dreaded, for it invariably means a Boche raid. Clear moonlight nights with a full moon are fine for lovers in a country that is at peace, but it may mean death for lovers in a country that is at war. But moonlight nights are beautiful even in war countries, with dim old cathedrals looming in the background, and the white villages of France, a huge château here and there against the hillside or crowning its summit; and the white roads and white fields of France swinging by. One forgets there is war then, until he hears the unmistakable beat of the Hun plane overhead and sees the flash of one, two, three, four, five, six, ten, twelve, fifteen bombs break in a single field a few hundred yards away, and the driver remarks: "I knew we'd have a raid tonight. It's a great night for the Boche!"

STARLIGHT AT FRONT

Then there is the starlight on No Man's Land, for the starlight is a part of the lights o' war just as are the moonlight and the star-shells and the little flash-lights and the range-finders and the bursting shells and bombs. But there are other more significant lights o' war.

There is the "Light that Lies in the Soldiers' Eyes," of which my friend Lynn Harold Hough has written so beautifully and understandingly. Only over here it is a different light. It is the light of a great loneliness for home, hidden back of a light that we see in the eyes of the three soldiers in the painting "The Spirit of Seventy-Six." It is there. It is here. One sees it in the eyes of the lads who have come in out of the trenches after they have had their baptism of fire. I have seen them come in after successfully repulsing a German raid and I have seen their eyes fairly luminous with victory, and that light says, as said the spirit of France, not only "They shall not pass," but it says something else. It says: "We'll go get 'em! We'll go get 'em!" That's the light o' war that lies in the soldiers' eyes back of the light of home. I verily believe that the two are close akin. The American lad knows that the sooner we lick the Hun the sooner he'll get back home, where he wants to be more than he wants anything else on earth.

Y. M. C. A.'s LIGHT

Then there's the light in the Y. M. C. A. hut, and from General Pershing down to the lowest private the army knows that this is the warmest, friendliest, most home-like, most welcome light that shines out through the darkness of war. It not only shines literally by night, but it shines by day. I have seen some huts back of the front lines lighted by the most brilliant electricity. Some of it is obtained from local power-plants, and some of it is made by the Y. M. C. A. Then I have seen some huts up near the lines that were lighted by old-fashioned oil-lamps. Then I have been in Y. M. C. A. dugouts and cellars and holes in the ground, up so close to the German lines that they were shelled every day, and these have been lighted by tallow candles stuck in a bottle or in their own melted grease. I have seen huts back of the lines away from danger of air-raids that could have their windows wide open, and I have seen the light pouring in a flood out of these windows, a constant invitation to thousands of American boys. And again I have seen our huts in places so near the lines that the secretaries had not only to use candles but to screen their windows with a double layer of black cloth, so that not a single ray of that tiny candle might throw its beams to the watching German on the hill beyond. I never knew before what Shakespeare meant when he said: "How far a tiny candle throws its beams." But whether it has been in the more protected huts back of the lines or in the dangerous huts close to the lines, the lights in the huts are usually the only lights available for the boys, and to these lights they flock every night. It is a Rembrandt picture that they make in the dim light of the candles sitting around the tables writing letters by candle-light. It is their one warm, bright spot, for a great stove nearly always blazes away in the Y. M. C. A. hut, and it is the only warmth the lad knows. Few of the billets or tents in France boast of a stove.

Two things I shall never forget. One was the sight of a Y. M. C. A. hut that I saw in a town far back of the trenches. It was in the town where General Pershing's headquarters are located. On the very tip of the hill above me was the hut. Its every window was a blaze of light. It was the one dominating, scintillating building of the town, a big double hut. When I climbed the hill to this hut I found it crowded to its limits with men from everywhere. The rest of the town was dark and there was little life, but here was the pulse of social life and comradeship, and here was the one blaze and glory of light.

The other sight that I shall not forget was up within a few hundred yards of the German lines. It was night. We were returning from our furtherest hut "down the line." We met a crowd of American soldiers tramping through the snow and mud and cold. They were shivering even as they walked. We stopped the machine and gave them a lift. I asked one of the lads where he was going. He said: "Down to the 'Y' hut in ——." I said: "Where is your camp?" He replied: "Up at ——." I said: "Why, boy, that's four miles away from the hut." "We don't care. We walk it every night. It's the only warm place in reach and the only place where we can be where there are lights at night and where we can get to see the fellows and write a letter. We stay there for an hour or two and tramp back through this —— (censored) mud to our billets."

And of all the lights o' war one must know that the lights of the Y. M. C. A. huts cast their beams not only into the hearts of these lads but across the world, and sometimes I think across the eternities, for in these huts innumerable lads are seeing the light that never was on land or sea, and are finding the light that lights the way to Home. And these are the lights o' war.

XIII
SILHOUETTES OF SUNSHINE

There is laughter and song and sunshine among our boys in France. Let every mother and father be sure of that. Your boys are always lonely for home and for you, but they are not depressed, and they are there to stay until the job is done. There are times of unutterable loneliness, but usually they are a buoyant, happy, human crowd of American boys.

Those of us who have lived with them, slept with them, eaten with them, come back with no sense of gloom or depression. I say to you that the most buoyant, happy, hopeful, confident crowd of men in the wide world is the American army in France. If you could see them back of the lines, even within sound of the guns, playing a game of ball; if you could see them putting on a minstrel show in a Y. M. C. A. hotel in Paris; if you could see a team of white boys playing a team of negro boys; if you could see a whole regiment go in swimming; if you could see them in a track meet, you would know that, in spite of war, they are living normal lives, with just about the same proportion of sunshine and sorrow as they find at home, with the sunshine dominant.

Some Silhouettes of Sunshine gleam against the background of war like scintillating diamonds and

> "Send a thrill of laughter through the framework of your heart;
> And warm your inner being 'til the tear drops want to start."

There was that watch-trading incident on the Toul line.

The Americans had only been there a week, but it hadn't taken them long to get acquainted with the French soldiers. About all the two watch-trading Americans knew of French was "Oui! Oui!" and they used this every minute.

The American soldiers had a four-dollar Ingersoll watch, and this illuminated time-piece had caught the eye of the French soldier. He, in turn, had an expensive, jewelled, Swiss-movement pocket-watch. The American knew its value and wanted it.

They stood and argued. Several times during the interesting transaction the American shrugged his shoulders and walked away as if to say: "Oh, I don't want your old watch. It isn't worth anything."

Then they would get together again, and the gesticulating would begin all over; the machine-gun staccato of "Oui Oui's" would rattle again, and the argument would continue, without either one of the contracting parties knowing a word of the other's language.

At last I saw the American soldier unstrap his Ingersoll and hand it over to the Frenchman, who, in turn, pulled out the good Swiss-movement watch, and both parties to the transaction went off happy, for each had gotten what he wanted.

One of the funniest things that happened in France while I was there was told me by a wounded boy one Sunday afternoon back of the Notre Dame cathedral. He was invalided from the Château-Thierry scrap in which the American marines had played such a heroic part. He was a member of the marines, and was slightly wounded. He saw that I was a secretary, and thought to play a good joke on me. He pulled out of his breast-pocket a small black thing that looked and was bound just like a Bible. Its corner was dented, and it was plain to be seen that a bullet had hit it, and that that book had stopped its death-dealing course.

I should have been warned by a gleam that I saw in his eyes, but was not. I said: "So you see that it's a good thing to be carrying a Bible around in your pocket?"

"Yes, that saved my life last week," he said impressively. Then he showed me the hole in his blouse where it had hit. The hole was still torn and ragged. In the meantime I was opening what I thought was his Bible.

It was a deck of cards.

I can hear that fine American lad's laughter yet. It rang like the bells of the old cathedral itself, in the shadow of which we stood. His laughter startled the group of old men playing checkers on a park bench into forgetting their game and joining in the fun. Everybody stopped to see what the fun was about. That lad had a good one on the secretary, and he was enjoying it as much as the secretary himself.

Then he said: "Now I'll tell you a good story to make up for fooling you."

"You had better," I said with a sheepish grin.

Then he began:

"There was a fellow named Rosenbaum brought in with me last week to the Paris hospital, wounded in three places. They put me beside him and he told me his story.

"It was at Belleau Wood and the Americans were plunging through to the other side driving the Boche before them. This Jewish boy is from New York City, and one of the favorites of the whole marine outfit. He had gotten separated from his friends. Suddenly he was confronted by a German captain with a belching automatic revolver. The Hun got him in the shoulder with the first shot. Then the American made a lunge with his bayonet, and ran the captain through the neck, but not before the captain shot him twice through the left leg. The two fell together. When the boy from New York came to consciousness he reached out and there was the dead German officer lying beside him.

"The boy took off the captain's helmet first, and pulled it over to himself. Then he took his revolver and his cartridge-belt and piled them all in a little pile. Then he took off his shoes and his trousers and every stitch of clothes that the officer had on, and painfully strapped them around himself under his own blouse. After he had done this he strapped the officer's belt on himself. When the stretcher-bearers got to him and had taken him to a first-aid and the nurses took his clothes off, they found the officer's outfit.

"'Say, boy, are you a walking pawnshop?' the good-natured doctor said, and proceeded to take the souvenirs away.

"This was the military procedure, but the New York boy cried and said: 'I'll die on your hands if you take them away.'

"He was a serious case, and so they humored him and let him keep his souvenirs, and when I saw them take him out to a base hospital this morning, he still had them strapped to him, with a grin on his face like a darky eating watermelon."

"What did you say his name was?" I asked.

"Rosenbaum," the boy replied. "Rosenbaum from New York."

"Say, if they'd only recruit a regiment like that from America, we'd send the whole German army back to Berlin naked," added another soldier who was standing near.

Then we all had another good laugh, which in its turn disturbed the old men playing checkers on the bench under the trees back of Notre Dame. But the soldier who told me the story added thoughtfully a truth that every one in France knows.

"At that, I'm tellin' you, boy, there aren't any braver soldiers in the American army than them Jewish boys from New York. I got 'o hand it to them."

"Yes, we all do," I replied.

This good-natured raillery goes on all over the army, for it is a cosmopolitan crowd, such as never before wore the uniform of the United States, and each group, the negro group, the Italian group, the Jewish group, the Slav group, the Western group, the Southern group, the Eastern group, all have their little fun at the expense of the others, and out of it all comes much sunshine and laughter, and no bitterness.

The Jewish boy loves to repeat a good joke on his own kind as well as the others. I myself saw the letter that a Jewish boy was writing to his uncle in New York, eulogizing the Y. M. C. A. He was not an educated lad, but he was a wonderfully sincere boy, and he pleaded his cause well. He had been treated so well by the "Y" that he wanted his uncle to give all his spare cash to that great organization. This is the letter:

"DEAR UNCLE:

"This here Y. M. C. A. is the goods. They give you chocolate when you're goin' into the trenches and they gives you chocolate when you're comin' out and they don't charge you nothin' for it neither. If you are givin' any money don't you give it to none of them Red Crosses nor to none of them Salvation Armies, nor to none of them Knights of Columbuses; but you give it to them Y. M. C. A.'s. They treat you right. They have entertainments for you and wrestlin' matches, and they give you a place to write. And what's more, Uncle *they don't have no respect fer no religion.*

"Yours,
"BILL."

Yes, France is full of Silhouettes of Sunshine. There was the eloquent Y. M. C. A. secretary. And while he didn't exactly know it, he too was adding his unconscious ray of light to a dull and desolate world.

The Gothas had come over Paris the night before, and so had a group of some one hundred and fifty new secretaries. The Gothas had played havoc with two blocks of buildings on a certain Paris street because of the fact that the bombs they dropped had severed the gas-mains. The result did have a look of desolation I'll have to admit. So far the new secretaries had done no damage.

Now there is one thing common to all the newly arrived in France, be they Y. M. C. A. secretaries, Knights of Columbus workers, Red Cross men, or just the common garden variety of "investigators," and that is that for about two weeks they are alert to hear the bloodiest, most drippy, and desolate-with-danger stories that they can hear, for the high and holy purpose of writing back home to their favorite paper, or to their wives or sweethearts, of how near they were to getting killed; of how the bombs fell just a few minutes before or just a few minutes after they were "on that very spot"; of how the raid came the very night after they were in London or Paris; of how just after they had walked along a certain street the Big Bertha had dropped a shell there; of how the night after they had slept in a certain hotel down in Nancy the Germans blew it up. We're all alike the first week, and staid war correspondents are no exception to the rule. It gets them all.

I came on my friend telling this crowd of eager new secretaries of the damage that the Gothas had done the night before. There they stood in a corner of the hotel with open ears, eyes, and mouths. Most of them were on their toes ready to make a break for their rooms and get all the horrible details down in their letters home and their diaries before it escaped them. They were torn between a fear that they would forget some of the horrid details and for fear some other fellow would get the big story back home to the local paper before they could get it there. When I came in, this nonchalant narrator was having the time of his young life. He was revelling in description. Color and fire and blood and ruin and desecration flowed from his eloquent lips like water over Niagara.

When I got close enough to hear, he was at his most climactic and last period of eloquence. He made a gesture with one hand, waving it gracefully into the air full length, with these words: "Why, gentlemen, I didn't see anything worse at the San Francisco earthquake."

In three seconds that crowd had disappeared, each to his own letter, and each to his own diary. Not a detail must escape. How wonderful it would be to describe that awful destruction, and say at the end of the letter: "And this happened just the night before we reached Paris."

Only the vivid artist of description and myself remained in the hotel lobby, and having heard him mention San Francisco, my own home, I was naturally curious and wanted to talk a bit over old times, so I went up to the gentleman and said: "I heard you say to that gang that you hadn't seen anything worse at the San Francisco earthquake, so I thought I'd have a chat about San Francisco with you."

"Why, I was never in San Francisco in my life," he said with a grin.

"But you said to those boys, 'I didn't see anything worse at the San Francisco earthquake,'" I replied.

"Well, I didn't, for I wasn't there. I just gave them guys what they was lookin' for in all its horrible details, didn't I? Ain't they satisfied? Well, so am I, bo."

This story has a meaning all its own in addition to the fact that it produced one of the bright spots in my experiences in France. That eloquent secretary represents a type who will tell the public about anything he thinks it wants to know about the "horrible details" of war in France, and facts do not baffle his inventive genius.

One characteristic of the American soldier in France is his absolute fearlessness about dangers. He doesn't know how to be afraid. He wants to see all that is going on. The French tap their heads and say he is crazy, a gesture they have learned from America. And they have reason to think so. When the "alert" blows for an air-raid the French and English have learned to respect it. Not so the American soldier.

"Think I'm comin' clear across that darned ocean to see something, and then duck down into some blamed old cellar or cave and not see anything that's goin' on! Not on your life. None o' that for muh! I'm going to get right out on the street where I can see the whole darned show!"

And that's just what he does. I've been in some twenty-five or thirty air-raids in four or five cities of France, and I have never yet seen many Americans who took to the "abris." They all want to see what's going on, and so they hunt the widest street, and the corner at that, to watch the air-raids.

One night during a heavy raid in Paris, when the French were safely hidden in the "abris," because they had sense enough to protect themselves, I saw about twenty sober but hilarious American soldiers marching down the middle of the boulevard, arm in arm, singing "Sweet Adelaide" at the top of their voices, while the bombs were dropping all over Paris, and a continuous barrage from the anti-aircraft guns was cannonading until it sounded like a great front-line battle.

That night I happened to be watching the raid myself from a convenient street-corner. Unconsciously I stood up against a street-lamp with a shade over me, made of tin about the size of a soldier's steel helmet. Along came a French street-walker, looked at me standing there under that tiny canopy, and with a laugh said as she swiftly passed me, "C'est un abri, monsieur?" looking up. The air-raid had not dampened her sense of humor even if it had destroyed her trade for that night.

[Illustration: The air-raid had not dampened her sense of humor.]

Another story illustrative of the never-die spirit of the Frenchwomen, in spite of their sorrows and losses: One night, when the rain was pouring in torrents, a desolate, chilly night, I saw a girl of the streets plying her trade, standing where the rain had soaked her through and through. Were her spirits dampened? Was she discouraged? Was she blue? No; she stood there in the rain humming the air of an opera, oblivious to the fact that she was soaked through and through, and cold to the bone.

This is the undying spirit of France. I do not know whether this girl was driven to her trade because she had lost her husband in the war, but I do know that many have been. I do not know anything about her life. I do know that there she stood, soaked through and through, a frail child of the street, plying her trade, and singing in the rain. The silhouette of this frail girl and her spirit is typical of France: "Her head though bloody is unbowed." Somehow that sight gave me strength.

The reaction of the German submarining in American waters on the boys "Over There" will be interesting to home-folks. When the news got to France that submarines were plying in American waters near New York, did it produce consternation? No! Did it produce regret? No! Did it make them mad? No!

It made them laugh. All over France the boys laughed, and laughed; laughed uproariously; doubled up and laughed. I found this everywhere. I do not attempt to explain it. It just struck their funny bones. I heard one fellow say: "Now the next best thing would be for a sub some night, when there was nobody in the offices, to throw a few shells into one of those New York skyscrapers."

"I'll say so! I'll say so!" was the laughing reply.

"Wow! There'd be somethin' doin' at home then, wouldn't there?" my friend the artillery captain said with a grin.

But about the funniest thing I heard along the sunshine-producing line was not in France but coming home from France, on the transport. It came from a prisoner on the transport who was sentenced to fifteen years for striking a top-sergeant.

One night outside of my stateroom I heard some words, and then a blow struck, and a man fall. There was a general commotion.

The next morning the fellow who struck the blow was summoned before the captain of the transport.

"See here, my man, you are already sentenced for fifteen years, and it's a serious offense to strike a man on the high seas."

"I didn't strike him on the high seas, sir, I struck him on the jaw."

The captain was baffled, but went on:

"What did you hit the man for?"

"He argued with me. I can't stand it to be argued with."

"But you shouldn't strike a man and split his mouth open just because he disagrees with you," said the captain severely.

"I just don't seem to be able to stand it to have a guy argue with me," he replied, not abashed in the slightest.

"Well, you go to your bunk. I'll think it over and tell you in the morning what I'll do about it," said the captain, and turned away.

But the man waited. The captain, seeing this, turned and said: "Well, what do you want?"

"All I got to say, captain, is that you mustn't let any of them guys argue with me again, for if they do I'll do the same thing over if you give me fifty years for it. I just can't stand it to have a man argue with me."

Silhouettes of Sunshine? France is full of them. There were the fields full of a million blood-red poppies back in Brittany, and the banks of old-gold broom blooming along a thousand stone walls; there were the negro stevedores marching to work, winter and summer, rain or shine, night or day, always whistling or singing as they marched, to the wonderment of French and English alike. Their spirits never seemed to be dampened. They always marched to music of their own making. There was that baseball game, when an entire company of negroes, watching their team play a white team, at the climax of the game when one negro boy had knocked a home run, ran around the bases with him, more than two hundred laughing, shouting, grinning, singing, yelling negroes, helping to bring in the score that won the game. Then there was that Sunday morning when several white captains decided that their negro boys should have a bath. They took their boys down to an ocean beach. It was a bit chilly. The negroes stripped at order, but they didn't like the idea of going into that cold ocean water. One captain solved the difficulty. He took his own clothes off. He got in front of his men. He lined them up in formation. Then he said: "Now, boys, we're going to play that ocean is full of Germans. You stevedores are always complaining about not getting up front, and you tell me what you'd do to the Germans if you once got up front. Now I'm going to see how much nerve you've got. When I say 'Forward! March!' it is a military order. I'm going to lead you into that water. We are going in military formation.

"'Forward! March!'"

And that company of black soldiers marched into that cold ocean water, dreading it with all their souls but soldiers to the core, without a quaver, eyes to the front, heads up, chests out, unflinchingly, up to their knees, up to their waists, up to their chins, when the captain shouted "As you were!" and such a hilarious, shouting, laughing, splashing, jumping, yelling, fun-filled hour as followed the world never saw. The gleaming of white teeth, the flashing of ebony limbs through green water and under sparkling sunlight that Sunday morning was full of a fine type of fun and laughter that made the world a better place to live in, and certainly a cleaner place.

War is grim. War is serious. War is full of hurt and hate and pain and heartache and loneliness and wounds, and mud and death and dearth; but the American soldier spends more time laughing than he does crying; more time singing than he does moaning; more time playing than he does moping; more times shouting than he does whimpering; more time hoping than he does despairing; and because of this effervescent spirit of sunshine and laughter his morale is the best morale that any army in the history of the world has ever shown.

Milton Keynes UK
Ingram Content Group UK Ltd.
UKHW011124180424
441376UK00004B/202

9 789357 963480